A. L. Rowse's copy

Boies Penrose

BOIES PENROSE IN HIS PRIME AS A LEGISLATOR

# Boies Penrose

## SYMBOL OF AN ERA

*by*

ROBERT DOUGLAS BOWDEN

Author of
"*In Defense of Tomorrow,*" "*Evolution of the Politician,*" "*Kid Colby,*"
etc.

NEW YORK
GREENBERG : PUBLISHER

PRINTED IN THE UNITED STATES OF AMERICA
BY THE VAIL-BALLOU PRESS, INC., BINGHAMTON, N. Y.

*This book*
*is dedicated to*

MIRIAM

# CONTENTS

PART   I.   BEGINNINGS . . . . . . . . *Page*  1

PART   II.   PENNSYLVANIA DAYS . . . . . *Page*  41

PART   III.   YEARS OF GROWTH . . . . . *Page* 101

PART   IV.   SENATORIAL COURTESY . . . . *Page* 127

PART   V.   THE NATION'S BOSS . . . . . *Page* 175

PART   VI.   TWILIGHT ZONE . . . . . . *Page* 223

INDEX . . . . . . . . . *Page* 267

# ILLUSTRATIONS

Boies Penrose in His Prime as a Legislator . . . *Frontispiece*

Vacationing in Florida in 1915 . . . . . *Facing Page* 42

In a Playful Mood . . . . . . . . . *Facing Page* 74

At the Wheel of His Yacht "Betty" . . . . *Facing Page* 74

At the Home of a Friend . . . . . . . *Facing Page* 106

At Palm Beach, 1915 . . . . . . . . *Facing Page* 106

Leighton C. Taylor, Secretary to Senator Penrose . . . . . . . . . . . *Facing Page* 170

*Part One*

**BEGINNINGS**

# BEGINNINGS

IN the autumn of 1877 a young giant from Philadelphia entered Harvard. He was six feet four inches in height, weighed two hundred pounds, had wavy black hair and steady black eyes that accentuated the insolent set of his mouth, and was possessed of such poise and self-esteem that those of less patrician mould thought of him as haughty. Though not yet seventeen years of age his olympian attitude toward the world in general and its puny inhabitants in particular had already become a part of the coloring of his daily life.

His name was Boies Penrose.

His is not the story after the American pattern of a poor lad fighting for and achieving great and glorious riches and success, nor, in the face of well-nigh insuperable obstacles, of winning fame by the oil-lamp and patched-jeans route, but a story of luxury, leisure, and laziness; of money and class; of arrogance of privilege and position; of noble ancestry. It is a story of great intellectual powers, keen observation, and monumental sloth; of neglected youth; of atrophied ambition; of idealism and disillusionment. Withal, it is a story of success—without benefit of ethics or acquisition; a success wrought of and measured in terms of cunning, boldness and determination; a success of power, riches, privilege, and of that lofty contempt which the patrician has for servile plebeians.

Boies Penrose in his own right is a fascinating study in this hectic business of living, but as a prominent figure in the whirlpool of politics, and as a symbol of all those forces which caused the whirlpool to go round, his life and times are absorbing. In the sweep of a single generation, from Lincoln to

Wilson, profound changes took place in American life—in her social pattern, her industrial triumphs, and in her economic warp and woof—which altered the direction and content of the American scene. And pivotal in all these changes was the political boss.

In the flux of circumstances and rapidly changing perspectives when life was unsettled and explosive, a thing of sharp contrasts, of high-lights and deep shadows, of blurred lights and crude nuances, the turbid conditions produced, as always, its own masters who partook of and reflected the crazy-quilt qualities of the times. Of all the masters exercising power in the half-century which furnishes the background of our study, Boies Penrose stands out with peculiar distinctness. He was the last and the greatest of those masters whom we call bosses precisely because he embodied most completely the characteristics of his time and was so completely the master of them.

One day in his second year at Harvard, Penrose said to his brother, Charles, roommate and classmate:

"You know, Charles, this place would make a first class dime museum."

"What place?" asked Charles, absorbed in his studies. Boies had finished his, as usual, before Charles got well under way and was now ready for something amusing to do.

"Why, all these rooms around the college and mummified professors. Not a damned one of them got any imagination. They got their jobs years ago, set in motion what ideas they had at the time, then ossified. They're worth a dime of anybody's money who's hunting a freak to look at."

"Be quiet, Boies, I want to work."

"Now take this man, Martin Van Buren, who made Jackson President," continued Boies, ignoring his brother's protest, "He had brains and used 'em! Bet he never wasted his time reading a speech some blighter made in Latin two thousand years ago. . . . But for years he was boss of the Democratic party."

"Maybe," agreed Charles, "but he didn't know much else."

"Who said so?" roared Boies. "That's what I had an argument about with Ted Roosevelt today. He sure is one conceited ass!"

"He must have won the argument," Charles jibed.

"That cock-eyed little runt win an argument with me? Hunh! Tell you what I'll do . . ."

"Cut it out, Boies, I've got to work!"

One who attempts to reconstruct the life of Boies Penrose cannot hope to draw in bold strokes a picture of a brilliant and colorful life rich in large achievement for his fellow man, nor one with a noble philosophy powerful in moulding succeeding generations. Color is there in abundance, but a detached and inharmonious color, in which achievement is not at first so apparent. One must search amidst the underbrush to find any signs of life and direction. He must seek in obscure places to find an imprint. But once familiar with the subtly brazen technic of all the little politicasters and of him who wielded such enormous power among them the large canvas becomes alive with minor characters that appear incredibly small and inconsequential, but they move in harmony and with a purpose. The purpose, however, is not theirs; they are the puppets that move in obedience to the desires of a master. Look behind the scenes if you would find the master! There he sits, Boies Penrose, in all the complacency of a powerful monarch, exhibiting a bored countenance as expressionless as a poker player facing either certain defeat or giant winnings. He plays as apt a brand of manipulation and with as finished a political technic as this nation or any other has seen.

He didn't invent the puppets; he merely learned that they were puppets and set them moving to his will. His personal contributions to the social and political welfare of the people if measured in terms of positive units of achievement were negligible, but he welded stout weapons out of the materials at hand and produced the type of strong discipline a people in an era of social and political transition demanded. No legislation of consequence bears the mark of his hand. His entire time and energies were spent in manipulating the thousands of puppets, large and small, that go into the make-up of a political machine, and in attendance upon the mighty industrial lords who collected the gate receipts of this strange puppet show and supplied him with ample funds to keep the show in full swing.

Boies Penrose was born the last day of November, 1860, at 1331 Spruce street in Philadelphia. His father was wealthy Dr. Richard Penrose of the Medical Faculty of the University of Pennsylvania and a direct descendant of William Biddle, one of the proprietors of the province of New Jersey, a friend of William Penn, and founder of the Biddle family of Philadelphia. His mother was of equally distinguished stock, reaching back to the household of Lord Baltimore, the founder of Maryland. We find the Penroses giving important help to the development of the colonies, and later of the Federal government, being particularly useful to Lord Baltimore, Benjamin Franklin, William Penn, Thomas Jefferson, and others in high official capacity. Family trees meant something real and mighty in Philadelphia in those days—the larger the tree the better the fruit. Boies Penrose considered himself the best possible fruit and took his own superiority for granted.

"I can trace my ancestry clear back to the first Adam" he boasted one day, half seriously, "and I wouldn't be surprised if I didn't inherit some of his original sin."

The Penroses lived in the Eighth Ward, the home of stiff

aristocracy. That is, the north half of the ward. Low brows and mean inconsequentials peopled the south half, and incidentally ran its politics. The north-enders, living in the shadow of Independence Hall and within the center of the patriotic universe, wouldn't even dream of contaminating themselves by dabbling in vulgar politics. Ever since the days of Jefferson public affairs had ceased to be a gentleman's game. It was now run by inferior folk and the hustings. The aristocratic Cadwalladers, Willings, Biddles, Drexels, and Penroses, were starchy enough to give stiffness to a whole nation. It has been said that they were the last to have their names printed in the telephone directory lest they be compelled, because of an exchange girl's blunder, to talk with people of inferior rank. Sarah Boies Penrose, mother of seven sons, of whom Boies was the oldest, was as regal as majesty itself, sternly suppressing every emotion and sentiment as befits great patricians. She instilled a like attitude in her sons. Births, deaths, great calamities were facts to be accepted, not to be reasoned about. Why make a fuss over something that is an established fact? Years later, upon the death of his mother, Boies sent a simple message to her closest friend.

"You may be interested to know that our mother was buried today." Not another word.

Illustrative of the typical Philadelphian attitude toward ancestry and "connections" is the story told by one who for many years headed a large personnel department whose task was to select young men starting in business careers and of scanning closely their letters of recommendation. So distinctive was the attitude of certain localities that it "stuck out all over" these written communications. This employer of young men boasted of his unerring accuracy in naming the city a young man hailed from merely by reading his letter of introduction.

If the applicant came from Boston his letter would read somewhat as follows: "Permit me to introduce Mr. Jones, who graduated with highest honors in the classics and political economy at Harvard, and later took a degree at Berlin. He speaks and writes French and German, and if you employ him I am sure his learning will make his services extremely valuable to you."

If the applicant came from New York his letter was like this: "The bearer, Mr. Brown, is the young fellow who took hold of Street & Company's Chicago branch a few years ago and built it up to a hundred thousand a year. He also made a great hit as Jackson & Company's representative in London. He's a hustler all right and you'll make no mistake if you take him on."

But from Philadelphia: "Sir,—allow me the honor to introduce Mr. Rittenhouse Palmer Penn. His grandfather on his mother's side was a colonel in the Revolution, and on his father's side he is connected with two of the most exclusive families in our city. He is related by marriage to the Philadelphia lady who married Count Taugenichts, and his family has always lived on Spruce street. If you should see fit to employ him I feel certain that his very desirable social connections will render him of great value to you." Not a word about his qualifications.

Boies never went to formal school till he had reached his teens, his training having been cared for by a private tutor. He was carefully guarded as to playmates but no effort was made to supply the lack of associations which such a gap forced on him. He was robust but inordinately lazy. Or, perhaps the lack of something definite to accomplish went for laziness. Although an aristocrat and a good deal of care being given to certain phases of his education he never learned discipline, for in one of superior breeding that would come of its own accord. Not the discipline of the social group but the discipline of a privileged class was his lot, consequently sloth and indifference crept in. Wholehearted play which is the portion of a normal boy during his early school years requires frequent subordination to a group. And that, Penrose never learned.

He was too lazy to be a leader among what few companions he had, for that required effort. Not having learned discipline he had no positive "morals" and never learned the value of them nor felt lack of them. Perhaps the greatest void in his early life was the absence of any social discipline. He was always to remain just a big lumbering, awkward boy, isolated from stimulating social contacts.

When his elementary training had been completed he entered the Protestant Episcopal Academy in Philadelphia, at which institution he was prepared for Harvard. During these preparatory years, the crucial years of adolescence, his tendency to aloofness developed which was believed to have been caused by abnormal sensitivity to sex. And the fact that he was usually segregated from those of the opposite sex added to this sensitivity. However, one may have reasons to modify that theory. It is more likely that his aloofness and sex consciousness, as well as his downright selfishness and laziness, were all resultants of the same causes—the barrenness of his social life and the lack of that happy camaraderie during early boyhood years which results from the rough and tumble contacts on the playground. But whatever the cause his tendency to aloofness and individuality increased. He was brilliant and cynical and taciturn, but his was the brilliance of skeptical and cynical superiority. When it became necessary to follow certain rules in games which he was persuaded to play occasionally he resented being told by an inferior athletic coach what to do, consequently he withdrew from the game, watched and criticized from the sidelines. His physique was calculated to gladden the heart of the most indifferent coach but he steadfastly refused to have any part in the rough and rowdy games played by obedient learners.

It became noticeable at about this time that he had an aversion to physical contact—with his own sex—that, as he grew older, became almost an obsession.

"Me? Have to brush against the messy, smelly bodies of *those* fellows?" he scorned one afternoon to the coach. "Whew! Count me out." In later years, it was said, he even refused to shake hands with people unless someone captured his by strategy, in which case he would go straightway to the washroom and use an antiseptic. In a politician that was a strange trait.

But his reluctance to shake hands with people on every appropriate occasion may be assigned to entirely different causes, as we shall have ample reason to explain later.

Boies and his younger brother, Charles, entered Harvard at the same time. Their mother, anxious that her sons associate with the "right" people and eschew all "improper" contacts, decided that it wouldn't do to trust her boys alone to find their way about in such a strange place; they might possibly tarnish the bright shields of their inheritance. So she arranged for her husband's elderly sister, Lydia Penrose, to go to Cambridge, assume the household duties of the bright Penrose youths, and act as their guardian. Young Boies snorted when he heard of the arrangements, but since his mother desired it and he respected her anxiety, he voiced no further objection.

"That's all right, mother. No doubt Auntie could use some further education."

"Nonsense! At her age? Your Aunt Lydia is going along to make a home for you boys and to look after you."

"Yeah!" said that young man stolidly. "As chaperons for Auntie, me and Charles, here, will show her some great times."

A house was rented not far off the Harvard campus and the four years of college for Boies Penrose got under way. It wasn't long before a chance acquaintance was invited or strolled into the sacrosanct headquarters of the boys, much to the annoyance of Aunt Lydia. But there was nothing she could do about it. The number increased. Hilarious sessions became common and, according to Boies' predictions, Auntie was shown "some great times."

But with all the stag parties and rowdy sessions, he never developed many friendships at college. He was such a severe individualist in all things that he had few real intimates. Being a chum to any one was entirely out of the question. He was not a strong fraternity man. He had no scruples against fraternities; he had no scruples against anything—except stupidity. It can be easily understood that in the rounds of daily campus gossip and activities he was never very popular. That met with his complete satisfaction. He didn't want to be popular, for that required him to be pleasant to others; he wanted to be deferred to. Why should others be pleased? Possibly no man in college life, and later in public life, had fewer friends than Penrose. That is, close friends. He was friendly or even pleasant to most people only so long as he could use them to his advantage. It was his dictum that friends were only maudlin sentimentalists and used their friendships as a cloak under which to ask favors. Most friends were stupid anyway!

Frequently it was remarked in utter astonishment that he had none of the suave, baby-kissing, back-slapping oiliness of the successful politician. Quite right! Nor could he warm up to the ordinary politician—except to use his vote and influence. He hated intimacy, yet he was one of the most successful politicians of his times. He was so utterly different from the standard brand of ward heeler or precinct choker as to appear of a different breed.

It is idle perhaps to speculate on what he might have been in other circumstances; on the appearance of the flower that could have been grown in more perfect soil, but one can't avoid being curiously interested in the many and varied influences which insinuated themselves into the boy's and young man's world to have caused him deliberately to turn his back on every opportunity which his superior background and his magnificent native ability assured. His mental endowment, as was his physical, was unusual but he purposely neglected both. There must have been some very definite reasons why at times he became so unbearably boorish in his attitude toward friend, foe, or casual acquaintance. He developed vulgarity in his appetites and habits and never gave a care as to results, nor what others thought of him.

"I do what I damn please in public or private, day or night," he told one of his political advisers who was urging him to be a little more discreet in his relations with women, "and not what the mob wants me to do."

That attitude was typical of Penrose throughout his years of maturity, becoming more offensively so as the years stole in upon him. One discerns in all this obtrusive bravado an attempt to conceal various shortcomings about which he was very sensitive. A partial explanation is that he never learned the art of meeting and associating with people as equals. As a matter of fact it was always as a superior facing an inferior, a condition of mind which made it impossible for friendliness to develop except for those few who took pains really to understand the man and like him in spite of his oddities. Then, too, one suspects him of suffering from certain disillusionments and disappointments from which he never entirely recovered. An overgrown adolescent in a sixth grade class, lazy, unprepared, and awkward, when called on to recite, fumbles and stammers in his stupid bluffing. The class giggles. The teacher waits patiently or prods firmly. The big lazy fellow, not prepared to recite and embarrassed at his shortcomings, resorts to sullenness or adopts the tactics of the bluffer or bully. He may insult the teacher or outrage the class in an effort to call attention away from his perfect ignorance of the assignment. This is his method of providing an alibi for his deficiency, a deficiency due to a lack of application and discipline. All his life Penrose was that overgrown schoolboy who preferred to win by bullying and playing to the gallery rather than by the development of merit, except in one thing.

In the first place young Penrose's home life was cultured but barren. There was really no formative influence there. The mother's time was too absorbed in the cold, formal ritual of maintaining the family pride and prestige among the subservient social butterflies to spend any of it catering to the whims of a belligerent boy. In his impressionable years of adolescence when a mother's kindness and understanding heart might have moulded almost any pattern desired, the young lad was left tragically alone, or consigned to the tender mercies of nurse and tutor. The father, apparently, was too absorbed in the pursuit of his profession and investments to be bothered about boyish pranks or indolence. Anyway, weren't the Penroses superior by divine right? They had no reason to be influenced by the censorious judgments of low plebeians.

Withal, however, there was something fine about the boy. He was inclined to be a dreamer. Tender romanticism was no more lacking in his make-up than in that of any other normal boy, but it was warped by neglect and killed by design. He was not allowed for one moment to forget that he was a Penrose, the salt of the earth, and therefore of high respectability. He must be a strong man and not give way to dreams and sentiment. In proportion as he drew more aloof from the crowd he developed an interest in reading books, a habit which never left him.

When, not yet seventeen years of age, he entered college there was absolutely no room for doubt in his own mind that he should receive the usual deference as a matter of right. Wasn't he entitled to it? But he didn't get it. It so happened that other aristocrats were to be found at Harvard and from as fine families as his, and in addition, most of them had had the advantages of social training and discipline. But not being able to meet them on terms of careless equality he failed utterly to "register" with them, a thing which he was never able to understand. It was a sore disappointment and sent him into a prolonged pouting rage during which time he drew more and more within himself. Very well! If they felt that way about it they could just go to the devil and he would go his own sweet way and sulk. And sulk he did! Consequently he was ostracized by most of the students, and during the greater part of his four years at college he was merely ignored by the leaders as just so much impedimenta cluttering up the premises. Fortunately his fine mind, not yet a victim of its later slothful corrosion, demanded exercise and that accounted for such excellent records in his favorite field, political science. In spite of chagrin, bitter disappointment, and exceptional arrogance, and his native laziness, the study of politics had a compelling interest for him and was the sum total of his excursions into the field of scholarship.

There is something about greatness that can't tolerate opposition. Fortunately for Penrose his opposition from an indifferent student body was just what was needed to stiffen the molds of his future action. He was a big man physically. He was a big man mentally. All these things he knew, but he wanted to make others acknowledge his bigness by exerting authority

and power over them. There was no better place to study politics in the raw than in college and he observed and absorbed
a great deal from the sidelines.

One day, out of pure deviltry, he tried his power in a way
that almost ended in physical combat, but he won. In his junior
year a student assembly was getting into action trying to whip
up some emotional froth when young Penrose got up in front
of that noisy, pushing, and pawing group and got their attention.

"Fellow students," he began solemnly, "while the chief
mourners are gathering I'm going to instruct you with a dis-
course on the ethics and pleasures of bull fighting. . . ."

A howl of laughter went up, and some protests, but he kept
the floor and finished his speech. It was an artistic as well as
a popular success, and he satisfied himself that he could master
the rabble.

That he had a recurrence of his tendency to dream is evi-
denced by the fact that he wrote two plays, one an overstuffed
romance, and the other was a robust Greek tragedy. With a
little encouragement he would have blossomed forth in verse,
but some of his classmates discovered the big fellow's secret
sins of the muse and made jokes about it, whereupon he went
into a rage and renounced it all. Such stuff was only sentiment
anyway, and he remembered to hate sentiment. Besides, his
literary efforts were doomed from the outset by his unwilling-
ness to apply his energies, and being too lazy to concentrate
for any great length of time on any construtive work he gave
over his hours more and more to reading and occasionally to
the effortless recreation of wine, women, and song.

Alternating these spells of sulkiness with periods of his favorite relaxation finally brought him, by the middle of his
senior year, to a complete loss of interest in his work and to
open rebellion against everything and almost everybody. His

college world in particular. At the midyear examinations of his senior year he failed miserably and would have let it go at that without a single regret had it not been for his father's intervention. The worthy Dr. Penrose caused his son to snap out of his lethargy long enough to take his examinations over, and with such success that he was graduated a few months later only second from the head of his class. His younger brother, Charles, was in first place.

The Penrose individualism and cynicism was influenced also from other factors, not the least of which was that of class distinction. The Penroses were among the First Families and therefore entitled to the patriotic homage of the newcomers and the less deserving masses. The rarefied atmosphere of the early patriots was the true seat of Americanism, and its inhabitants claimed greater rights in making laws to guide others. Superiority was preserved and fostered by holding aloof from low plebeians and in being exclusive and dignified, for there was never any doubt about the noble First Families. But now, in these latter days, to see power and authority become the common possessions of illiterates and foreigners and vulgar traders was entirely too much for them to accept. Certainly they couldn't be expected to co-operate with such people; it would compromise every revered principle. All these things impressed themselves on Boies Penrose as facts and not as theories. Why quarrel with facts? His one interest in life being an absorption in politics he fell quite naturally into the study of it at college, and he ended his career there with a class oration about Martin Van Buren. From that day on his interest in politics was at white heat and, although times changed and methods were modified, his interest never lagged. For that reason he looked about him to see what politics were doing to his own city and his own times. He learned much that surprised him, much that invoked his well-known cynical snarl, but he also found much that intrigued him enormously. From that day forward his interest and activities applied to politics were purely pragmatic. There was no place for theory and idealism in politics.

The rulers of state and national politics in 1876 were an incalculable distance from those who had ruled two generations earlier. Power had slipped from the hands of our Jeffersons, Madisons, Clays, Websters, Bentons, Calhouns, and Sumners into those of our Quays, Camerons, Hannas, Yerkes, Morgans, Mellons, and Crokers. Even to the Buck Devlins and Iz Durhams and Dave Martins. The one central question which dominated Penrose was not how power was used but how it passed from one user to another.

If we examine a little more closely into the social and industrial soil in the national garden after 1865 and take a look at the seed so extravagantly planted in it, we may discover other influences which brought to full blossom such sturdy and truly representative politicians as Boies Penrose.

Born in 1860, he was in his impressionable teens before the end of that saturnalia of hate conducted by the Honorable Thaddeus Stevens and Company, a period which Claude Bowers calls the "Tragic Era." Before he had reached his middle twenties he was forsaking a puny attempt at law practice for the cesspool of saloon-dominated ward politics in one of America's most corrupt cities. This was in the early eighties, the decade which Schlesinger says marks the Nadir of National Disgrace. He was in all essentials a by-product of that awful struggle between two economic systems fighting for supremacy which culminated in the Civil War. Only incidentally was slavery, as a moral and ethical question, an issue in that struggle. It was essentially a fight between two economic philosophies. The slave economy had placed in the hands of three hundred and forty-seven thousand persons the complete ownership of approximately three and a half million slaves as well as nearly all the real estate in one corner of a continent stretching all the way from the Delaware to the Rio Grande. It owned, absolutely the politics of every village, city, and state in that section, and dominated national politics. It chose thirty of the sixty-two members of the United States Senate, ninety of the two hundred and thirty-two members of the House and, what is more significant, controlled all the important committees in both branches. It controlled five of the nine members of the Supreme Court, and under the spoils system the upholders of slavocracy penetrated and almost absorbed every branch of the Federal government. In these circumstances it was not to be expected that such a system would give up its power without a struggle.

But the slave economy operated in a limited territory on land of constantly diminishing fertility. Being a static economy it was inevitable that sooner or later it should be overtaken and crushed by an industrial era drawing its sustenance out of an ever-expanding area, a growing surge of immigration and free, cheap labor, and diversified living conditions based on a thousand sources of income.

All these sources of wealth could be tapped and exploited only through control of the machinery of government which at that time rested solidly in the bedrock of the southern aristocracy. The task was to break it loose and use it to satisfy the hungry thousands in the industrial North and East. The lusty industrial era based on technological power, crying for recognition, could grow to robust maturity only through high tariffs for favored industries, on subsidies and bounties and commercial coddling. Indeed, the fundamental causes of the war rested in just these things. Andrew Curtain, the War Governor of Pennsylvania, in a speech shortly before his inauguration, said not one word about abolishing slavery but he had a great deal to say about "the vast heavings of the heart of Pennsylvania whose sons are pining for protection of their dearest interests. . . . This is a contest involving protection and the rights of labor. . . . If you desire to become vast and great, protect the manufactures of Philadelphia."

Fifty years later when Penrose was at the height of his power one of his followers asked him: "What's going to be the issue of the campaign this time, Boies?"

"Hell, man! Have you arrived at the age of discretion and don't know that there's always only one question worth making an issue out of? Protection! Protect the great industries of this State and you start dollars flowing out to every home in the State. We make that possible because we control the government at Harrisburg and at Washington. We intend to keep that control."

After the South seceded the protection began with surprising vigor. The war was only a few months old when profiteering in war contracts and supplies began to smell unpleasantly and soon became a national disgrace. Gossip and authentic news reports began to reek with stories of graft. And all these stories pointed unerringly toward the War Department inhabited by Mr. Lincoln's Secretary of War, Simon Cameron, who, by the way, was the first real boss of Pennsylvania politics. He was well versed in all such things as padded contracts, petty graft, and bonuses. In fact the political machine which he constructed for Pennsylvania was such an efficient bit of mechanism that it still renders excellent service. From Cameron to Vare it never bogged down completely. It kept "Old Kickapoo" Cameron, efficient swindler of Indians, in the United States Senate twenty-four years, and his son, Donald Cameron, in the same seat as his successor for twenty years more. And in 1897 the senatorial toga graced an ardent chauffeur of the Cameron machine, Boies Penrose, who continued in power another quarter of a century.

Theodore Roosevelt, fresh out of Harvard in June, 1880, one year before Penrose was graduated, decided to enter politics. The Republican Club of his ward, spoken of, because of the aristocratic nature of its inhabitants, as the "Silk Stocking District," was as difficult of entry as if it had been the most exclusive yacht club. That was long before the day of ballot reform and controlled primaries. The political party was still treated as a private corporation, a close corporation at that. An outsider was not admitted to its inner circle until his complete pedigree was known. Highbrows and reformers were kept severely out—except as occasional window dressing. So when young Teddy announced his intention of joining the 21st District Republican Association, his parents and friends scoffed and laughed him out of countenance. Politics "were low" they told him and not to be bothered about by the upper classes. The organizations were all run by saloon-keepers, horse-car conductors, and the riff-raff in general, and not by anyone whom he would ever meet in the business and professional world. That being the case, he told them, he determined to be one of the governing classes, as it was clear that none of his friends and acquaintances ever belonged to that class. He soon learned that the peasant-saloon keeper and his social world had become the center of the political world. The gentry, the well-bred, the first families, stood aloof from the vulgar business of running the country.

Boies Penrose, at about the same time in Philadelphia, was learning that identical conditions prevailed there. "You had to break into one with a crowbar," he said, speaking of political clubs, but he soon learned how to wield the crowbar. He learned these things so thoroughly and from such authentic sources that his new associates were astonished. It had already been decreed, by the powers that decree such things, that Penrose was to become that which carried the utmost in respectability and prestige—a Philadelphia lawyer. Accordingly it was arranged for him to study law in the offices of one of the leading firms in Philadelphia, Wayne MacVeagh and George Bispham. MacVeagh had been named Attorney-General in President Garfield's Cabinet. This was a magnificent opportunity indeed for any aspiring young man to serve an apprenticeship at law. But young Penrose's ambition, if any, died the moment he entered that somber respectability.

"Too damned dull!" he grumbled.

But the dullness of his professional duties by day was never allowed to dampen his ardor for bright evenings. Closing time would usually find him on his way to his favorite saloon where the social atmosphere was more to his taste. Likewise the food and drink. He was a prodigious eater. When he craved a real he-man's dinner—and that was at least once a day—he didn't go home to get it. Although the home on Spruce street was well stocked with servants and food, his father was a doctor and "the family was always on a diet." Instead he preferred to become the focal point of a couple of well-trained waiters who understood what a satisfactory meal was like. A whole duck, or its equivalent in weight and fineness plus all the side dishes plus a quart of good liquor, constituted the first course.

And he must have the proper atmosphere for thorough enjoyment. He didn't want to be stared at, he said, "through gold-mounted lorgnettes by a lot of overstuffed females, nor pushed around by rigid waiters in dress suits." Democratic? No! Far from it. In fashionable dining rooms he would be treated as an equal, or ignored; in Jerry's side street ale house or Frozen Bill Conery's oyster house he was treated with commendable deference, so the latter type of place got his patronage. There he met the owners and managers of political gangs and learned their technic, and learned to know the camp followers as well as the strong-arm executives of the boss's orders. To the latter he was always Mister Penrose. Wasn't he one of God's elect? Hadn't he come down from the upper reaches of polished society, of the gentry and the patrician, to be one of them?

Quite likely the dinner, before it was half finished, took on the appearance of a ward political convention with all the small fry among the vote-scalping and ballot-box stuffing gentry eagerly soaking words of political wisdom from this twenty-two year old sage. He knew his political science from books; they knew theirs from the gutter, and he was as eager to talk to them as they were appreciative of the artistocrat's attention. During all these days he was the prober, the seeker, the practical research student mastering all the processes of political control, and learning them from the bottom up. Besides, it was pleasant business. If some of the political Big Boys of the ward made a chance appearance they were lucky to get so much as a nod from him. He studiously ignored them unless they exhibited the proper humility and respect.

When he tired of eating he stalked down the street a few blocks to Middle Alley or Soap-Fat Alley, or perhaps to the Madame's Palace of Pleasures where feminine accomplishments and decorum were elastic enough to permit an evening of thorough entertainment.

The next day the business of law occupied him—when he got to it. His schedule was as irregular as his conduct. He never possessed an alarm clock so his day began whenever he awoke, whether that happened to be 10 A. M., or 2 P. M. The requirements of his professional pursuits received the same studious application which he gave to getting to them on time. Nevertheless he was admitted to the bar in 1883 and at once began the practice of law as a member of a law firm composed of himself, Edward P. Allison, and S. Davis Page.

It was during his attempt at the law profession that he had his next flirtations with authorship. In fact the first money he earned after coming to the bar was earned by writing a dissertation on white elephants. P. T. Barnum opened his circus season that year in Philadelphia and his latest sensation was a white elephant. At least Barnum said it was white. Skeptical persons declared the elephant had a skin disease and that Barnum, as usual, was fooling the public.

One of Barnum's men, a speculative gentleman, accepting Barnum's own classification of the beast, began looking for someone who could write a descriptive and "authoritative" article about white elephants, their habitats, their place in religious history, and so on. Some jokester sent the man to attorney Penrose. The showman began eagerly to outline his wants to Penrose saying he would pay $25.00 for a readable account of Mr. Barnum's latest zoological sensation.

"Say no more," Penrose cut the man short, "I'll write your damned elephantine article for you. It'll be readable, too."

The article was written that night. Boies Penrose broadened the theme so as to cover elephants of all colors—black, white, brown. The article was printed in pamphlet form and sold, by Barnum of course, all over the United States.

"What did you really know about white elephants?" a newspaper friend asked him.

"I knew just about as much about white elephants as I did the black ones," he replied without a flicker of a change of countenance.

At the request of the Johns Hopkins School of Historical and Political Science he wrote a history of his own city, "Philadelphia, 1681 to 1887." It was during his work on this study that he produced the original charter of the city given by

William Penn. It had been "lost" for more than a hundred years in the Biddle family's archives. His second book, "History of Ground Rents in Philadelphia," ended his career as an author. The practice of law was not so exacting.

It is not quite correct, though, to say that he ever practiced law. The records of the time fail to reveal any hint of his participation in any sort of legal activity whatsoever—except to stay out of it—for his time was absorbed in matters of more importance to him, such as getting acquainted with the work of ballot manipulations, and the manipulators. If one wanted to get on in politics these worthy gentlemen and their methods were well worth knowing. The testimony of one of them is typical.

"The fraud of an election," he stated, "does not really begin till night, then in dozens of precincts where the judges and election clerks of both big parties have been 'fixed' we put down just what returns we want, or may need to insure us a majority. John Smith may have 500 votes in a given precinct, but if John Smith is the man we want to defeat we knock off two ciphers and credit him with five votes. This is cheaper than hiring 500 'Indians' to cast illegal ballots. With a five-cent pencil we can in five minutes cast more votes on paper than 5000 citizens can cast in a ballot box in a whole day."

But "fixing" all these judges and clerks requires money and a purpose, and who should be the logical persons to pay all this money? Who else except those who derive the greatest benefits? And who are they? Certainly not the politicians. Penrose learned very early in his twenties, as did Theodore Roosevelt, as every student of American politics has long known, that the politician, from the hardboiled wielder of pick handles and machine guns on decent but luckless citizens on election day to the respectable ward boss, to the mayor of cities (or the maker of mayors), to the persuasive manipulators of national conventions and dictators of national legislation, are not the ones who get the rich rewards of politics. They get the meager crumbs of petty graft, such as a few dollars on "expense accounts," or small contracts, immunity in the courts, gratuitous checking accounts, campaign funds, and continuance in office. Occasionally one of them gets in on the big money—the Tweeds, the Vares, the Bill Thompsons, the Abe Ruefs, to name only a few—but they are the exceptions to the general rule. The real Capones of political strategy seldom hold office. They are too busy in the business world watering stock, forming paper mergers, arranging huge foreign loans, jacking up tariffs, and the like, but they insist on having friendly officials elected merely as mechanics of the machine and chauffeurs to run them and do errands for the industrial lords. When these "friendly" officials are elected they obediently vote millions of dollars in franchises, sewer contracts, public utility monopolies, power rights, and many sorts of "services" for the public at enormous profits to themselves and enormous expenses to the taxpayers whose votes are nearly always futile. The boss's set purpose is to find out what the Big Boys want, then he dictates to the smaller fry how and in what manner to satisfy those demands.

The system in Pennsylvania, from Cameron to Penrose, has been so uniformly successful that it is sometimes spoken of as the Pennsylvania "Idea" and has been copied widely. A recent political comment has pointed out that Former Secretary of the Treasury, Mr. Andrew Mellon, is the perfect figure-head of this system of government.

"Of course he does not buy votes himself. But he has never concealed his own belief that it is the chief function of the State to favor the accumulation of wealth in comparatively few hands, and the chief task of practical politics, from his own point of view, is to keep, at any price, the Republic true to its mission. For this purpose the Republican party in particular is liberally financed by the businessmen of the country, and its continuation in power is fortified by a vast array of moral and social entrenchments.

"The actual control of government is lodged nominally in a majority of voters. Notwithstanding the insidious and overwhelming propaganda, the legal bulwarks, the general prevalence of money motives and standards and the elaborate machinery for the disqualification and frustration of the opposition, the voters now and then will be led astray. It is necessary, consequently, in an emergency or in event of a struggle within the dominant party for control, to be prepared to buy votes. The Republican machine in a state such as Pennsylvania is designed as a regularly constituted agency for purchasing votes and the other vehicles of political power. Its recent performance is a frank revelation of the kind of politics which a hybrid democratic plutocracy needs in order to serve and exercise its domination over society.

"The tacit verdict of American public opinion is that if the triumph of Mellonism demands a little extra expense at elections, it is worth what it costs. This clearly is a state of affairs in which the power, the responsibility, and the moral values of society are vested ultimately in big business and its parasites."

Boies Penrose was determined to know every detail of the methods by which the above very desirable state of affairs could be brought about, and according to him there was no better place to learn about it than right in the midst of it. He knew all about political science. Learned it at Harvard—out of books. But that was theory, he said, and about as far removed from realities as down is from up. Consequently his law practice suffered while he spent the greater part of his time mastering a political technic that proved itself immune against law. Not that he disliked law; merely that he was indifferent to it and considered it a maze of trivialities invented to perpetuate the mastery of the ruling classes over the ruled. Of course it didn't apply to noble patricians like himself, but he had to know something about it in order to apply it more profitably to the large body of plebeians and also to keep away from its sting. But as for using law as a profession he wouldn't give so much as a second glance at the most promising client in the universe. If clients wanted to seek his services, all well and good; if not, ditto. If they came he would give grudgingly of his time and talents, unless some vote-stealing artists or political dopesters used their privileged profession to demand an audience, in which case the clients would be shooed unceremoniously out and the remainder of the day would be given over to matters of greater political import. He didn't have a very high opinion of people who used the law either defensively or offensively. Only a bunch of jackals! Later, when he had forsaken the practice of law altogether for politics he explained:

"I'd rather dictate to damned fools than to serve them." In less than a year from the time he was admitted to the bar he quit it for politics.

He began his active political career as campaign manager for LaBarre Jayne, candidate for a seat in the city council to represent the 8th ward, and as we have seen, this ward was the political home of two broadly distinct groups of citizens separated on a geographical basis into North-enders and South-enders. The latter were the ruling class and consisted of dive-keepers, loafers, pool room owners and habitues—in short the riffraff of the underworld, held together and bossed by Good Time Buck Devlin. He was the political czar of the 8th ward and boasted that he "could deliver results (in any election) to order." Plenty of orders came from franchise seekers, and various and sundry gentry devoted to "the easy life," for him to fill. At his word brothels were kept open or were closed, gambling thrived or—otherwise, and the ward's vote in the city council could always be "fixed" to order. The North-enders, reaching to the sacred precincts of Independence Hall, were pious aristocrats of wealth, position, and birth, and paid heavy tribute to their rulers, the lowly South-enders. They raised dignified objections, of course, and they fumed and scolded, but Buck Devlin went right ahead year after year and filled all the sacred offices of government with whom he pleased. All the leading business and professional clubs were in this ward, too, but somehow they just couldn't get hold of the rascals who were robbing their tax pockets. The Manufacturers Club, Union League Club, the Philadelphia Club, the Markham, etc., included in their lists of membership not only the patriotic flag bearers of the Republic but the social arbiters and the business brain trust of the city as well, but they were helpless to do anything about the Devlins, the Izzy Durhams, the Dave Martins, and a score of others. Of course elections were held usually at the most inconvenient times and the overlords of business were away on vacations or business and far removed from the battle of the ballots. No matter. They were voted regularly by the obliging Mr. Devlin. And not only were the absentee voters recorded as voting—for Mr. Devlin's choice of course—but the monuments, the cemeteries, vacant houses, and the like, never lost a vote. The purpose of the machine was always to have at the close of election day a safe margin of ballots for the machine slate. To carry out this purpose many devices were used, or were at hand to be used in case of necessity, for a political machine's power rested always on its ability to deliver a victory when most needed. Ballot box stuffing was one familiar method of winning an election. On one occasion these Philadelphia artists stuffed the ballot box in a certain precinct so full of ballots before the polls opened that when the first voter arrived he couldn't get his ballot into the box except by pounding it in with his fists.

Young neophyte Penrose, like Theodore Roosevelt, had decided that he would become a member of the governing class but unlike the latter he refused to court the favor of the group he wanted to join. In the most favorable circumstances joining a political club in those days was no easy matter. They were not in the habit of sending out nicely engraved invitations to would-be bosses, especially to the socially elite graduates of Harvard. To work himself up like any other cub was irksome to Penrose, so he decided to make a flank attack. If Buck Devlin of the 8th ward was not sufficiently impressed by the Penrose superiority that was Mr. Devlin's hard luck. In an adjoining ward, the 7th, a rival boss, jealous of Devlin's growing power, possibly was the first person to appraise the young upstart at anything like his true worth and to encourage him along his course. His name was Israel W. Durham, better known as Iz, or Izzy, highpriest of 7th ward politics. Izzy Durham had no special love for a representative of the intellectuals but he had a very pronounced dislike of Devlin's methods and success, hence he was delighted to have a chance to defeat the latter's candidate by aiding the rival. Besides, he boasted that "he could spot a winner every time."

Boies Penrose in Philadelphia and Theodore Roosevelt in New York marked the entrance of the college man into politics. Ordinarily a college graduate who brazenly jumped into the middle of a boiling campaign as Penrose did would have been hooted and jeered off the lot by the crude gentry who never approached any nearer college than the nearest side-alley gutter, but with Penrose it was different. To the illiterate

and unregenerate rabble of Philadelphia's underworld the fact
that Penrose was a college man was of minor importance compared with the knowledge that he was a member of the blooded
aristocracy, had wealth, brains, and was of formidable size.
They stood in awe of him, a fact he quickly sensed and made
use of. The managers and bosses had some misgivings about
"these college kids, fresh from their books and pink teas," in
the realm of politics, but being able to look ahead they accepted
Penrose as a forerunner of other educated politicians in the
future.

Curiously enough the efforts of young Penrose were en-
listed in behalf of the so-called reform element. Any person
in those days who worked for a change in government was
listed as a reformer. Mr. Jayne, a neighbor of Penrose and
therefore of the genteel element, a lawyer and therefore
worthy of the highest respect, was selected by the Committee
of One Hundred to defeat the machinations of Devlin and his
gang. And bright young Boies was asked to aid in the political
funeral of Mr. Devlin. The Committee of One Hundred was
composed of the business and social bigwigs of the city, which
meant they were all members of the Union League Club, and
similar pillars of the existing order. They thought it would
be a fine gesture to ask the son of Dr. Penrose to help their
efforts.

Would he help the cause? Would he? Would a sponge
soak up water? . . . He swallowed the opportunity at one
gulp. He plunged into the campaign in his slow, drawling, but
intelligent way and gave a convincing demonstration of his
practical knowledge of political procedure. It was all delightfully simple. First, you had to know all the tricks of the gang;
Penrose had learned them; then you had to get out the vote
and see to it that only those persons legally entitled to vote

should be allowed to do so; Penrose did all that, too. Finally, only such votes as were actually cast should be counted; Penrose saw to that. A very big order!

Boies selected the toughest place in the ward and calmly announced that he was going to conduct an honest election. He knew the element he was dealing with, as well as the technic they used, and he was prepared to meet them. He instructed watchers in all the other polling places what to expect. Secretly he had compiled his own list of eligible voters and no one who was not on that list was allowed to get in sight of the ballot box. The gang swarmed in on him early in the day, as had been expected, but they didn't stuff any boxes. His great strength and cool courage were equal to the combined strength of several of the hoodlums and he acted with energy. There were a few bruised heads and bloody noses, but no illegal ballots were cast that day.

"For the first time in the history of that polling place," according to Walter Davenport, "nobody not entitled to vote got by. Mr. Devlin, entering the conflict with empty ballot boxes (Penrose had seen to that, too) into which none but valid ballots were permitted to be dropped, magnanimously conceded defeat several hours before the election was over, celebrating it with free beer, fine sportsman that he was. Instead of sulking in Denny (B'God) McGowan's, his headquarters for the day, he summoned a squad of his lustiest skull wallopers and called on young Penrose, who was, at that moment, seeing to it that none but the privileged voted.

" 'Boy-iss,' said Mr. Devlin, 'I extend the right hand of fellowship and welcome. Let's be friends. In case there's any trouble at the counting I've brought with me a few extra strong billy-goats who'll stand by you and break the legs off anybody you point out. If you care to step over to Frozen

Bill Conery's this evening I'd like to talk to you about this great wave of reform that has spread over the upper end of the noble Eighth.'

"Mr. Jayne won by 58 votes and Mr. Devlin, a strong advocate of the theory, 'If you can't beat 'em, join 'em,' dropped everything to sell this new star in his political firmament to the machine which, in spite of what had happened in the noble eighth, had survived and still reigned.

" 'Is there any job you'd like?' asked the jocular Mr. Devlin of young Penrose. 'The giving of it is not mine but I wouldn't be surprised if—'

" 'I'd like to be mayor,' said Penrose solemnly.

"Buck was a bit staggered, but asked innocently:

" 'Of Philadelphia?'

" 'Yes.'

" 'Would you be willing to wait a while?' asked Mr. Devlin.

" 'Of course.'

" 'That's the boy,' cried Mr. Devlin approvingly. 'Don't be in too much of a hurry. That great man himself, the Honorable Matt Ka-way will be in the city the day after this and if it was me I'd—' "

But Penrose had other plans and did not at present meet "that great man, the Honorable Matt Ka-way." As a matter of fact, Boies felt that advice and assistance from any source was superfluous and just so much energy wasted. He could stand alone.

But that excellent young man was not a reformer. He had no sympathy with reform and despised reformers. To him anybody who whined of injustice and immoral conditions was a weakling who, being both cowardly and weak, tried to get other weaklings like himself to abolish that which he was afraid to have for his very own. Common and inferior folk had always been a subject and therefore an obedient clan!

They had to please their feudal lords and went to great exertions to train themselves in humility and self-denial, in a manner of daily living that made them fit subjects to be ruled! If one of them perchance so far forgot himself as to get helplessly drunk he brought down upon his head the wrath and scourge of the master who stood to lose profits by his subject's waywardness! Any levity was frowned upon. But if the master folk chose to wallow in drunkenness and debauchery that was merely being masterful! It was nobody's business! The Ten Commandments were drawn up to hold the masses of servants in line and make them humble! The masters of course could ignore them at will! Only servants enjoyed their sins in private!

To the end of Penrose's life he acted consistently with the above views. There are several things to be remembered in this connection, however, in order that the whole picture may be seen. Penrose had an intellect that was of a different pattern from those of most of his associates. Whether preparing for the bar examination or a test in one of his college subjects he could apply himself to it for about one-fourth the time required by the average student and still make a better mark. He could read and digest four times as much in a given time as the average man, consequently he had more time on his hands, much of which he chose to spend in his own way instead of with the mob. Drinking was quite common in those days, as always, but it was more secret. Like divorce, for example, which acknowledges a state of unhappiness which formerly society decreed be concealed. In the eighties and nineties if a lady exposed an ankle she was immodest. Penrose had no more carousals than a good many other men, but his conduct was exposed for all the world to see. And especially, for a man in public life not to be circumspect every time he turned a corner, was a signal for everybody to pronounce horrified exclamations. Penrose stripped himself of hypocrisy to the point of nakedness.

When his political associates, alarmed at the openness of his jousts with levity, reminded him that his public exhibitions were harming him and his party, that after all a professional man was a servant of the public and therefore should be discreet, if not circumspect, he replied: "Public servant, hell! Who said so? Servants are not rulers, are they? I'm running my office and I do as I damn please. It's none of the public's business what I do."

If John Citizen, argued Penrose, observes the sparkling splendor of a good drink but is restrained by instinctive repressions from tasting its delights he is merely confessing his lower-class status and surrendering to an invisible master. But in secret he will go out and taste all the sins in the catalog. Because he is too cowardly to step forward openly and take what he wants he snoops around and denounces others for enjoying and possessing what he himself is afraid to possess. Furthermore, he wants to destroy all delights and encourages other snivelling incompetents to join him in destroying things and reforming people. Bah! Hypocrits! Every reformer on record was a failure or a cast-off! Therefore, being frank and open, if he felt the absolute necessity of rest and relaxation in his favorite lady's boudoir, though it be in mid-afternoon with the whole world watching his goings and comings, he followed his bent.

The rank and file of Pennsylvanians in Penrose's days of apprenticeship held similar notions to his about such things as personal and class relations and those who were the masters of them. "A Pennsylvanian's land was his kingdom," R. W. Kauffman tells us. "He held it in fief to an emperor vaguely personified in the Commonwealth, to whom he paid certain taxes and to whose general laws he was amenable; but he was its liege lord. Notwithstanding its religious precepts the Society of Friends was composed of feudal-minded individuals, and the Friends' neighbors were their political brothers. . . . Later immigration was slow to affect the old order. The Germans that came to us in the 19th century were largely law-abiding Western Catholics; so were the Irish and so have been most of the Italians who followed them. . . . It was the employers themselves that made the change. . . . The feudal holdings of life's necessities were so large a proportion of the nation's store that the holders could have maintained their positions (except for the radicals). . . . We Pennsylvanians were the satisfied subjects of paternalism: Stevens died on a Tuesday in August of 1868; the Lancaster County Republicans' primary for the Nomination of a Congressman had been set for that Saturday; no candidates would present themselves while the body of the representative whom they loved remained above ground; the voters knew that he was dead, yet, when the ballots were counted, it was found that every one had been deposited for Thaddeus Stevens.

"The Cameron Dynasty, father and son, ruled us to our taste. Quay was their heir; even his factional rivals like now to think that no other state has produced so great a master of political strategy. Then Penrose came, Harvard magna cum laude, holder of the bequeathed power magna cum laude, too. But at his death there was the fear of the radical. . . ."

The radical which they feared was none less than certain citizens who felt that the feudalistic dynasty had outlived its day of usefulness and who wanted to mould the weapon of party power into an organ more responsive to the desires of the subjects of the feudal lords.

With victory safely tucked away for the estimable Mr. Jayne, through the efforts of his campaign manager, Doctor

Penrose's fine young son, the better element in the 8th ward basked in pride and happiness. The future took on a rosy tint and held great promise for good clean government. They had found a leader!

Penrose sniffed a little disdainfully when he heard that. He was pleased in a sort of superior way, but for an entirely different reason; he had found the road to power and he determined to follow it—in his own way. As for the reformers whom he had aided, he flipped a snap of his fingers and dismissed them.

Why? He was shrewd enough even then to observe that any true reform would strike a fatal blow at economic privilege. He was a proud member of a class privileged by birth and tradition. But his diminishing group had little or no control of affairs. The other privileged group, the money kings, had acquired their privilege by securing political favors. Without control of the party machinery they could not hope to maintain their privileged status against the just demands of the underprivileged public. But to encourage the reformers in their honest fight which would benefit a wider public would mean weakening the prestige and power of the master group itself, and Penrose instinctively fought to maintain the rights of his class.

"The better element," he said, with a wry twist of the mouth and with a little higher tilt of his nose, "don't know their way about in politics. They think people want to be good. Well, they don't. One day in the week is about all the goodness most people can stand. They want somebody who'll go ahead and do things. As for ethics and morals, leave all that to the preachers and the 'nice people' who haven't anything else to do."

If one is tempted to pass off such an attitude as that of a cynical youth who hadn't yet found his proper balance one must remember that Penrose grew up and developed his political bent in a period, the 'seventies and 'eighties, when political processes and business codes of morality had dipped to the lowest level in our history. A. K. McClure, who ended sixteen years of continuous service in the Pennsylvania Legislature in 1874, wrote: "During that period venality in legislation reached its tidal wave. I saw it in every phase, and many times supported measures when I knew that a considerable portion of those who were voting with me had demanded and obtained a price for their votes. . . . The corruption of legislators was not, as a rule, for the benefit of individuals, except as they might profit by the grand enterprises which they planned for the vast resources of the commonwealth. They were halted by the legislative corruptionists and compelled to bow to their demands or leave the state. . . . For years during that period I saw the private memoranda of the leading lobbyists, in which the name of every senator and every representative was recorded who could be corruptly influenced in legislation, and I have seen in that record as many as 70 of the 100 members of the House and more than 20 of the 33 senators. . . ."

If the writer of that article could have looked in upon the scene at the end of the century, nearly thirty years later, he would have changed his statement that venality had reached its tidal wave in the seventies. Only a start had been made at that time. In the easy slang of a later period, "you ain't seen nothin' yet!" That tidal wave swelled into its mightiest proportions toward the closing years of the century and lashed out most destructively, perhaps, in the largest cities in America, but it spread into every hamlet and byway of the nation, subsiding gradually during the years that followed leaving revelations of its destruction in almost every community, even as late as the year of 1933. Among those few who harnessed the power of this tidal wave and directed its benefits, who had the foresight to grasp the opportunities of that period of chaos and collect its driftwood, was Boies Penrose.

Shortly after this February election in 1884, Penrose's mother died, and for some months thereafter he took no part in politics. In late summer he and his younger brother, Charles, who later became a celebrated surgeon, went to the Rockies on a hunting trip. Not only did he hunt for big game but he indulged his fondness for nature. He spent much of his time tramping through the mountains studying the flora and fauna of the regions. He covered most of the Rockies and Sierras doing more nature study than hunting, thus making further concession to his otherwise submerged idealism. It was said by those who knew him best that perhaps no person in the United States had a more complete knowledge of the country's animal and plant life than did Penrose.

While he was away Garfield and Arthur were making mighty efforts for the Republicans trying to continue the party in power at Washington. Penrose was only mildly interested in all this, being content to push his ambitious claims to power in his own way from the smaller political units upward. Devlin cared nothing for national affairs so long as he could manage his part of Philadelphia. Quay, Pennsylvania's nimble boss, was intensely interested in both the national election and the state elections. Nor did he neglect the petty affairs of small wards. He had many favors to give to obedient henchmen in all these small places, which he did with the utmost finesse. He listened sympathetically to Devlin's account of the reform movement in the noble 8th and of the masterful young leader who had so neatly defeated the old gang at their own game.

"Buck," he said, genuinely interested, "I wouldn't be surprised if he can't be a lot of help to us. Just give him a bigger field for his talents."

Devlin proceeded at once to find a bigger field for the absent Penrose. He called a few of the boys together in the back room of Denny McGowan's saloon and held a political convention to nominate a candidate for the State Legislature. Ward conventions were simple affairs in those days and delightfully free from the tom-tom beating of the larger conventions which had to create a lot of froth for public consumption. Only a few of the chosen inner circle, to whom the boss could safely intrust credentials, were allowed to attend. And they magnanimously consumed great quantities of free drinks and voted for the high-minded gentleman suggested by the boss. Thus Boies Penrose became the great standard bearer of the grand old party at the November election, that is, for a very small section of Pennsylvania. Of course Mr. Penrose would be duly appreciative of the high honor thus accorded him and in the future would do the machine's bidding with becoming humility.

Nomination of anybody on the Republican ticket to fill any sort of office was tantamount to election, for no one but a hopeless boob would vote for a Democrat. Not in Philadelphia. So when Penrose returned a few weeks before election and was appraised of his nomination he accepted the news in typical Penrosian calm and prepared to go to the State Capital as a member of the law-making tribunal of Pennsylvania.

*Part Two*

PENNSYLVANIA DAYS

VACATIONING WITH HIS BROTHER AND FRIENDS
IN FLORIDA IN 1915
(*Above*) The cottage at Stuart
(*Below*) On one of his fishing trips off St. Lucie

## PENNSYLVANIA DAYS

On a raw January day of 1885, Boies Penrose, age 24, a newly elected member of the State Legislature from Philadelphia, arrived in Harrisburg. He had been nominated without his knowledge and elected without his assistance. He was to represent a portion of Philadelphia whose constituency embraced the ultimate extremes in social and economic strata and all the shadings in between. That is, theoretically. Fortunately for Penrose he knew the difference between theory and practice. In reality he was only the errand boy from his district for the thoroughly corrupt, arrogant, and domineering Philadelphia Republican Organization, and he was not especially thrilled at this step in his fortune. It didn't even call for an extra drink in celebration of his victory. In fact it hadn't been a victory at all, for being a member of the Pennsylvania Legislature in those days carried no special honors with it, and his election was merely a step from one place to another in the necessary process of reaching a goal which embodied the sum total of his life's ambition—the mayoralty of Philadelphia. That required but one thing—the approval and support of the ward and district bosses who counted the ballots on election day. No other special qualification was necessary. He was now an accepted member of that corrupt robber band known as the machine, and in a subtle way was being disciplined by it. For the present he would accept its orders and obey its edicts; later he would give the orders. True, he had defied and ignored the political overlords in the 8th ward, but that was by way of demonstrating his fitness to belong to it. He had delivered a winning vote for his candidate; what more could be asked? No higher praise can be heaped upon a politician than the acclaim which comes to him for delivering victory at the polls. The efficient Republican Organization, under the local leadership of Goodtime Buck Devlin and ably assisted by the affable Iz Durham, was quick to recognize his worth and ability and took him unto its bosom.

There was something almost incongruous in the spectacle of a member of the most aristocratic group in American life descending from its high social sphere of the roof-garden to crawl through the rat holes below the basement floor. More important still, he made it his business to associate with the rats. He realized that the inhabitants of the roof-garden, should the structure collapse, would fall with the building, but the rats could scamper unnoticed to other holes. The collapse would rate great headlines in newspapers but the rats would usually be overlooked and forgotten.

As Penrose reached maturity certain characteristics, certain traits and habits of mind, became set, molded in forms of behavior-patterns, and they became more clearly identified with him as time went on. These rules of conduct or behavior, if they may be called such, were not consciously adopted by him but grew out of the nature of the man himself. They seemed almost instinctive. For convenience I shall group them as follows:

1. *His first, last, and only love was politics.* From college to the day of his death the game of politics consumed every hour of his life and every affection of his being. He never got married nor came within any remote prospect of it. He had no time nor room in his affections for anything except politics— as a love to be wooed; as a game to be played; as a career to be followed; as a profoundly important business to be promoted. He became a master craftsman in all these pursuits, and he did it not by accident or good fortune but by constant study and

the application of shrewd judgments. His aim was not to create "great friendships" nor to make enemies. He made a few of each. He was never vicious nor mean nor little nor sentimental. If occasionally a private in the ranks got plugged or "did time," it was just too bad, but it was no particular concern of his. It was all a part of the game.

2. *He had an unshakable obsession of greatness.* From the days of his early youth there was in his mind a firm conviction that he was "born to be great," to exercise power and direction over his fellow man. It was not arrogance, nor achieved merit, nor delegated authority, but inherited superiority of class and brains, of bigness. He always wanted to be a "big" man, a he-man among lesser men. He despised weakness and trivialities. He spent during his years as senator at Washington a hundred thousand dollars a year of his own funds to maintain all the appurtenances of greatness, superiority, bigness. Rules were not made for him—rules of health, of "moral" conduct, rules of suave society—nothing counted with him but a steadfast adherence to the one dominant motive of his life: to be powerful in the field of politics.

3. *He was boldly, consistently, beautifully, free from hypocrisy.* It was an ingrained conviction with him that whatever he chose to do night or day, and in whatever manner, was nobody's business but his. He hated men who "voted one way and drank another," men who criticized him for doing openly what they did in secret. He hated petty graft and snivelling incompetents who resorted to it. In commanding legions of office seekers, cheap politicians, vote-getters, petty chiselers, and grafters, there were no rules—only the objectives of control. He had an uncanny ability in judging people, and he was satisfied in his own mind that the great masses of people engaged in getting on in politics were of the above type. Hence he was never impressed by the over-friendliness, hand-

squeezing, and back-slapping affected by most of them. They would double-cross you if it suited their purpose! So why be a hypocrit and encourage them at their game?

His office was arranged with this in mind: his big desk was drawn at an angle across one corner of the room with just enough room behind it for his chair. When he was there the space was filled so that no zealot could get near enough to him to whisper in his ear, pound him on the back, or look over his shoulder; people had to talk to him from across his enormous desk. Those whom he learned to know and trust never had any criticism to make about his unfriendliness. And he never misused or double-crossed a friend.

4. *He had no scruples or "set" principles to live up to or avoid.* A general conducting a campaign must let no petty obstacles interfere with his larger plan of action. He had no inhibitions. He demanded and realized absolute freedom in whatever action he engaged.

From our high peak of detachment, some fifty years removed, we may now view in broad panorama the American scene at the time young Penrose entered public life. Municipal government was testing the caliber of the American people in self-government. "Almost everywhere," states an observer at the time, "when it was found that the original government would no longer meet the issues of the day, newly incorporated cities were provided with miniature replicas of state and national governmental machinery. The essential differences between a municipality and a commonwealth were not yet grasped, and too late people found that the type of organization which they considered ideal lent itself admirably to the manipulation of local politicians." Except occasionally in the case of "one of the boys" like Tweed the general public was appallingly apathetic toward municipal affairs. With the constantly and rapidly shifting of frontiers most people had never achieved more than a parochial view of politics. And since one man's vote was as good as another's, one man's opinion was as good as the other fellow's. Anybody could fill offices in a democracy, a doctrine that was taken full sail by the demagogue. Penrose realized this.

"What we need in this country most," he said one day in conversation with a reformer who was condemning all demagogues, "is not fewer demagogues but somebody to rule the demagogues and make them toe the mark."

With the advent of electricity applied to machinery city councils became the focal points for great swarms of privilege seekers; not service-givers. Demagogues multiplied like mosquitoes in a swamp.

All these things and their possibilities absorbed the attention of Penrose above all else, sometimes to the disgust of his law partners. One day shortly after his admission to the bar his law firm was delving into an important case, and a few veteran attorneys had been called in for consultation. Young Penrose sat around in bored silence listening but taking no part in the deliberations. Suddenly one of them asked him if, in his opinion, they had sufficient grounds for appealing the case.

"What do you think about it Boies?"

"I think it's a damned shame."

"What's a shame?" Allison asked in surprise.

"All this talent going to waste," Penrose replied in his drawling, tenorish voice. "You men have been sitting here for three hours quibbling over whether 'the' is more legal than 'a,' and nothing comes of it, while a few nitwits down in Denny McGowan's saloon run the city and pass up millions in franchises because they haven't brains enough to get 'em. Humph! . . ."

"But this is the way to become a good lawyer," one of them replied.

"And respectable, I suppose? A corpse is nearly always respectable. . . . Why, look at my father, for example! He and a couple of his friends own enough of the city railway stock to boss the company and the City Council, too, but instead he spends his days out at the college exhibiting pickled stiffs and respectable skeletons to a lot of lazy louts that don't know the difference between a pelvis and a reflex. Bah!" he snorted in disgust and unfolded himself to his full height.

"What do you suggest we do about it, Boies?"

"Suggest? Nobody ever got anywhere suggesting. You gentlemen stay here and masticate the law while I go down and join the nitwits."

"Happy Valley," a term applied by some impressionable journalist to the American scene at the time, made inspiring to him by the sounds of the industrial army on the march, in reality proved to be "Death Valley"—death to the hopes and ideals of millions. Penrose was impressed by the scene, too, but his impressions stirred different emotions. He saw the chaos and confusion and uncertainty as assets with an enormous book value ready to be made real by anyone who could seize upon all that uncertainty and harness it for a definite purpose. He preferred to keep the masses uncertain and confused, for in their extremity finally they would respond all the more readily to the soothing palaver of the garish demagogue.

Into the Valley came Edwin Markham who saw and pitied "The Man With the Hoe"; into it came Boies Penrose who had seen "The Man With the Hoe," and his million brothers but passed them by with haughty contempt, for in the center of the Valley he observed the delectable mountain of economic power with political Zeus astride the top, and forthwith he decided to abide with the Great One.

In Harrisburg Penrose dutifully and unobtrusively found a seat in the rear of the House on the Republican side and watched the process of manufacturing laws. He hadn't occupied that place many weeks till he confirmed an earlier notion about lawmakers that their first duty was not to make laws but to learn to be good rope jumpers. He also realized that once one becomes expert at jumping the rope the managers of the show keep one in that role. Immediately Penrose, therefore, decided to swing the rope instead of jump it, for as a wielder of that useful instrument one had infinite possibilities.

A glance at the personnel of the Pennsylvania Legislature in 1885 gives one an impressive, if not altogether inspiring, picture of political material in the Keystone State. That was especially true of the House. The Senate, perhaps, was unusual in the number of brilliant men who composed it. But that group was an exception instead of the normal type. Typical of a majority in the Senate, and House when Penrose entered the Legislature, was one William R. Andrews, better known generally as Bull Andrews. He was a big sturdy fellow with a rotund face, full chest, and with more hair on the back of his neck than on the top of his head. His mustache was distinctive for its volume and wing-spread, and was of the variety that enabled its owner, when rushed for time, to soak up a cup of coffee at breakfast and drink it at leisure on the way to work. He was called other names besides Bull Andrews, some of them lacking in elegance, but included in the more enticing ones was that of "Asparagus Bill." Being a very popular and efficient State Senator, he was appointed on a number of investigating committees, more appropriately, junketing trips. There was much in need of investigation in Pennsylvania in those days and the Senate liked nothing better than taking care of these needs. On one of these trips Bull was having considerable difficulty in making up his expense account. It wouldn't "add up" quite right so that accounts balanced as he wanted them to, so, to even matters a little better he added one more item: "To asparagus—$1000." His account was honored with pleasure, for such little tricks as that afforded no end of amusement among the hard-worked law makers in Harrisburg.

Bull's greatest success in the Senate was as efficient lobbyist for the Standard Oil Company. Lobbying has changed a lot since those days when brawn, brazen contempt for legal hindrances and a complete absence of morals were the prime requisites. Bull had all these qualifications. His physical proportions were impressive, his voice was a huge bull-frog bellow, and his demeanor entirely innocent of suave pleasantries or subtleties. You either jumped to obedient attention when he roared or you had to be told just where to "head in at." He was possessed of none of the arts of a leader, and was miles behind either Quay or Penrose in downright agility of mind. But he was successful at "bulling things through," hence his success as a lobbyist.

His most satisfying job at Harrisburg, however, was as messenger boy for Quay. Not only that, but he was Quay's body guard, personal secretary and adviser. When Quay nodded his head Bull went into instant action.

Last but by no means least among the coterie of politicians who made up Penrose's active world in Harrisburg was the masterful ringmaster of them all, Matthew Stanley Quay. He was at that time the chairman of the State Republican Committee and reigned as the big boss of Pennsylvania politics. He was, at the time Penrose entered the Legislature, past fifty, a little more than twice as old as the latter, and physically not nearly so impressive. He was a smallish man, being five feet six inches in height, and wiry, but with a finely moulded head which gave the impression of massiveness. He had a broad, prominent brow, eyes wide apart, one of which was slightly miscast. In dress he was inclined to be sloven and extremely careless. For a number of reasons, some very apparent, he was never a recognized member of the ruling senatorial oligarchy. He was too much of a free lance in looking after Pennsylvania and Matt Quay.

The two men had met only casually before but they were well acquainted with each other's career. Quay had made it his business to learn all about aspiring young politicians and to give or withhold his approval before said aspiring young politician began to aspire.

These two men were worlds apart in appearance, personality, and characteristics, but were one in ultimate purpose. Quay was a classical scholar, quoting freely from the Latin. He was a prodigious reader. Kipling called him the best literary critic in America. He was a minute observer of people, a delver into their motives, and had boasted that he could read most people better than they could read themselves, which accounts for his ability to deal with men and win them. He stood on common ground with all sorts and conditions of men. To a reformer he was devout, quoting the Bible as occasion might require (he was a son of a minister); to a tyro in politics he gave advice and counsel; to an opponent he was anything from granite obstinacy to lying compromise. Penrose presented one side to all people. He made no effort to fawn and simulate. His was the merit of never calling upon God to be his partner in winning votes. Quay would frequently desert and betray one circle of political associates, if it suited his purpose, and form an alliance with a new one. Suave, ruthless, cunning, gentle, cold-blooded, brainy, utterly untrustworthy—Quay was all that, and withal a scholar.

For more than fifteen years he had been absolute boss of Pennsylvania politics. That is, with the possible exceptions of

Philadelphia and Pittsburg. When, therefore, a bright new member of the Legislature arrived at the capital his first duty was to call in appropriate humility upon the grand sahib to receive the big chief's appropriate orders and blessings. If the member had the misfortune to be a Democrat his call was not met with rousing welcome but he called nevertheless; he had to before he could have his "passport visaed" entitling him to enter the Capitol and have his name entered on the roster of members. In his tender regard for the welfare of the Commonwealth Quay made it a point to have hotel accommodations reserved for the new members in advance of their arrival. He wanted to know at a moment's notice just where to find them. In a legislative session orders are likely to be issued any time of day or night.

Now, it so happened that Mr. Penrose, upon his arrival at Harrisburg, ignored his plain duty to call upon Mr. Quay. He also ignored Mr. Quay's hotel accommodations. Oh, he would see him some other time, to be sure, but there was no hurry about such things. It so happened also that Bull Andrews, an ideal example of a legislative rope jumper, not only was an obedient puppet to Mr. Quay but his body guard and personal secretary as well. So when Penrose failed promptly to observe the proprieties of a call upon the Great One himself, Bull Andrews was so outraged at this insult to his master that he sought out young Penrose to lay down the law to him in plain language and to demand of him who in hell he thought he was anyway. Boies merely looked down in his usual bored manner at the angry man and said:

"Sorry I've never had the pleasure of an introduction to you. Good day!"

So saying, he pushed the smaller man aside and stalked on about his business. The flabbergasted Mr. Andrews rushed back to his master to suggest a quiet and discreet murder, but the shrewd boss, being an excellent judge of human nature and behavior, forthwith despatched a formal invitation to the Honorable Boies Penrose to dine with Matthew Stanley Quay.

From his early maturity in the 1850's to his death in 1904, Quay was, except for a period of about three years, the occupant of public office in Pennsylvania. The Civil War Governor, Andrew Curtain, whom the youthful Quay slavishly served, placed him in a strategic position of power in Republican councils in the State, and from that time to the last years of his life he dominated, save one, the selection of every treasurer of the State. And from that point of strategy he made and unmade legislators, governors, mayors, United States Senators, and Congressmen. He named pardon boards and colored their decisions.

The anti-riot bill was a case in point. In the summer of 1877 railway strikes spread throughout the eastern half of the nation. A serious riot over the labor question occurred in Pittsburg in which more than a score of lives were lost and property damage ran into the millions. The courts gave the Pennsylvania railroad judgment against Allegheny county for the sum of two and a half million dollars. An anti-riot bill appeared in the State Legislature which would have given the Pennsylvania railroad four millions out of state funds rather than out of the funds of Allegheny county. One wonders why, in the first place, if the claims could be settled for two and a half millions, there was any necessity of appropriating four millions. It was not much of a secret to those who knew the situation that the extra one and one-half million represented graft to leading politicians. And why make the state pay what was legally the burden of one county. It was thought to be a lot easier to deal with the subservient legislators than with county authorities.

In the process of trying to make this bill into a law charges of bribery were made against several members of the Legisla-

ture. Five of the accused pleaded guilty and others were convicted. The penitentiary was already opening its doors to receive them. The interesting feature of the matter was that before sentence was formally passed Quay had the Board of
Pardons convened and pardons agreed upon for such as should
be convicted. Within a few hours, therefore, after the Court
spoke, pardons for all were signed, sealed, and delivered, and
the guilty men released.

Due quite largely to conditions which produced the strike
in the spring and summer of 1877 and the methods of handling
them the entire Republican state ticket was defeated in the
fall election. But two years later they snapped back into
power.

William H. Kemble, state treasurer of Pennsylvania in the
early sixties, coined the famous phrase, "Addition, division,
and silence," which instantly came into popularity as the working creed of the state Republican organization. The law then
forbade a state treasurer to succeed himself, but that was soon
changed, adopting the privilege-seekers' code of ethics—*If the
law stands in the way, change the law!* In order to secure favorable action by the Legislature on a shady project of fi-
nancing street railways out of state funds, then turning the
franchises over to the Honorable William H. Kemble, it was
necessary to consult Mr. Quay, a power even then to be reckoned with in state politics. Mr. Quay would be delighted to
assist—for a consideration. Said consideration was not only a
voice in the street railway project but a firmer alliance among
all the contending factions for control, with himself as the
central arbiter.

His stronghold thereafter was the State treasury. Though
he actually occupied the office only two or three years in the
following quarter of a century or more, he dominated the se-

lection of the man to fill it as well as every major decision and action which that man took. For more than thirty years it is said the little red colonial treasury building that stood at the north end of Capitol Hill at Harrisburg was the real source and seat of state government. In the stately Capitol that reared its dome alongside, governors and legislators came and went. But the power that made them and the money that often elected them came from that little red building. When it was torn down the "system" moved with the treasurer to the new building; for the system was continuous.

When Penrose thumbed his nose at custom and failed to make a prompt call upon the mighty Quay, the master politician at once realized the value of the young Philadelphian and at once set about winning him to the Quay standard. Penrose proved to be both an apt and an interesting pupil.

In his own good time he accepted Quay's invitation to dinner. Among many peculiarities about the young man's habits one concerned the matter of dress. It was said that on his first call on Quay one shoe was laced with a corset string. At another time he wore a new outfit from tip to toe, but neglected to wear a collar. He affected to enjoy going about the streets wearing clothes that accentuated his already enormous size. The usual ensemble consisted of a coat several inches too long, a peach-basket hat of extraordinary proportions, and shoes that were too large for him. But when he arrived at Quay's hotel for the dinner he was dressed in perfect taste, almost to the point of fastidiousness.

"I've ordered dinner for the both of us," the host said in his usual patronizing manner, as the two sat down to dinner. "If you want something in addition we'll get it."

Penrose looked at the dainty meal before him. "Call a waiter," he said promptly.

When the waiter arrived he began receiving an order the like of which he had never heard before. Penrose first ordered another highball and then an oyster cocktail.

"Not a couple of wizened little fellows in a glass, mind you!" he cautioned the waiter, "but some big fat ones—a dozen at least . . . bring plenty of sauce and a plate of celery . . . Then this fried chicken looks all right—bring me both halves . . . And a couple slices of this roast prime ribs . . . A quart of your best wine, and—"

Quay eyed his guest and the waiter alternately and with increasing interest—and dismay. Finally the host could stand it no longer and began joking about such an order. "Perhaps we had better ring for another waiter," he suggested.

" 'T won't be necessary," was the reply. "Just employ this one full time."

"A noble profession you're entering, Mr. Penrose," Quay suggested, by way of being affable.

"Lot of hokum," was the prompt and stolid reply.

"Oh, don't you like it?"

"Well, you see, Mr. Quay, mostly they're a lot of nitwits who make a great noise that nobody knows the meaning of including themselves. The welfare of the people hasn't got a chance."

"That's where you're wrong, young man. The real interests of the people are looked after by a few leaders like myself, and a few steering committees. They decide on policies and bills, then these, ah—nitwits vote them into laws."

"I thought so," growled Penrose. "Then why not send them all home and save the state money?"

"Ah, but they are our public opinion—after they vote into law what we tell them to. They form a sort of smoke screen for us leaders who have to have a little privacy."

"A noble profession, Mr. Quay, for the leaders."

"But had it ever occurred to you, Mr. Quay," Penrose said between courses, "that public opinion may change sometime and look into your methods a little?"

"You may remember, young man," Quay said in utmost courtesy, "that I was doing business at this same stand the day you were born."

"And thriving on the same old hokum," grunted Penrose.

"It isn't hokum," stoutly defended Quay. "It's all a necessary part of getting things done. Don't you see?"

"Times are changing, Mr. Quay. Look at all the new inventions, all the new industries, and such things, springing up! They are going to be run by young men with new ideas and they'll demand new political set-ups. . . . It's all plain to me."

"I'm sure we can work together, Mr. Penrose," said Quay patronizingly. "Stick to me and we'll do things!"

"Very well! . . . Call that waiter again!"

Penrose, with becoming modesty, took his place at the rear of the Republican side of the House and gave his attention, for the first few days, to the conduct of the machinery of lawmaking. It wasn't very long, however, till he began to give vent to his contempt for the whole lot of the representatives of the people. Most of them he thought were stupid and talked too much for the little they said. He was looked upon from the very first as Quay's aid, which fact irked Penrose no little. At once he determined to challenge the relations between the two by making a direct frontal attack. Luckily for him there was a weapon ready at hand in the proposed new charter for Philadelphia. Penrose's predecessor in the House, William C. Bullit, had sponsored a bill which would give the City of Brotherly Love a new and up-to-date charter. Under the old charter the mayor was nothing more than a puppet ruler in the hands of a dozen powerful feudal lords, or more modernly speaking, ward bosses and councilmen. The chief executive of the city was helpless in a maze of an extraordinary distribution of powers among the ward representatives, but there was nothing he could do about it. The proposed charter would concentrate all those powers in the mayor's hands and drastically curtail the powers and activities of petty ward bosses and councilmen. Of course all the little bosses fought it tooth and nail and through Quay effectively blocked it. The latter had never felt any too sure of his influence in Philadelphia and he was anxious to do what the bosses there wanted. That was much safer than openly antagonizing them. Penrose saw possibilities in this situation and went at once to Quay and announced casually that he would immediately move to get action for a modern charter for his home city.

"The Bullit measure would about fill those requirements!"

Mr. Quay's jaw dropped in astonishment at the boy's audacity and effrontery. Hadn't he just defeated that bill once?

"Mr. Penrose," he said finally, in some irritation which he had difficulty in controlling, "you may realize after a while what some of us older leaders have realized for years that an organization such as ours must have discipline. It must have a leader, and that leader must be followed!"

"Quite true, Mr. Quay, quite true," answered Penrose unperturbed. "An organization must also use brains."

"What?"

"Brains! It don't require much."

"What do you mean?"

"I mean that any organization such as the great Republican party in Pennsylvania will run along for years without much happening to it. But if it keeps making the same mistakes year after year it will soon find itself out in the cold."

"You think I've made a lot of mistakes?"

"Mr. Quay, you are not very strong in Philadelphia, are you?"

"Who says I'm not strong in Philadelphia?" demanded the granite Mr. Quay.

"I live there," replied Penrose calmly, "and know my way about."

"I've elected every man I want from there," was the somewhat chastened reply.

"There are half a dozen aspiring bosses down there, Mr. Quay, fighting each other. If they ever decide to join forces and fight you, they'll make you look like last Easter's hat."

"And how will this Bullit measure help me in Philadelphia?"

"Look here, Mr. Quay," Penrose replied: "I'd supposed you would have waked up to your own interests by this time. All those little fellows down there are old-timers, they're getting old, and they're already slipping. Most of them are ignorant saloon keepers. They're satisfied with a buttered cracker once in a while. 'T won't be long, though, till some of these younger bucks will be crowding all the old boys out, and, believe me, this new crowd won't be satisfied with a buttered cracker. They'll demand the whole meal and give you the cracker. It'll be a damned sight easier to control one mayor than a dozen. Besides, the reform element is growing all the time. They demand blood. Give 'em a new charter and they'll quiet down thinking they've won a great victory. Then we can go right along year after year electing the mayor we want who will have all the power instead of being just a figurehead."

Penrose didn't add that it was his one ambition in life to be that mayor. Of course he didn't want his hands tied by any ward heelers when he was mayor.

The Bullit bill came to a vote in the House May 12, 1885. On that day we observe the twenty-four year old member from Philadelphia leading the fight for its adoption and displaying a leadership more nearly approaching that of statesmanship than anything connected with his public life in following years. A number of the members from his own city were bitterly opposed to any change in the city government of Philadelphia, but instead of confining their opposition to the merits of the issues under discussion descended to denunciation of those persons who were supporting the measure. They, most of them, were members of long standing, and their statesmen-like qualities had decayed with the years—a disease quite common among certain types of public officials. Young Penrose had entered the House less than five months prior to this incident and displayed more or less an indifferent attitude to the varying tides of what went for oratory. He was content to remain in the background till he heard the bald hypocrisy and demagogery of the opposition, then he sprang into action with a speech that was a powerful rebuke to those opponents who "stooped to wash dirty linen in public." He refused to invoke personalities and launched out in a masterful defense of the proposed measure. He reminded the House that the City of Philadelphia had for two generations been under the absolute control of the Gas Trust and that unless something could be done within a short time the renewal of their lease would make their rule permanent. The proposed charter would place the control of the Gas Trust in the hands of the Mayor and Council. In answer to the charge that the new charter would make a mayor all-powerful, he replied that the power of impeachment could be used at any time to remove an incompetent mayor.

"Whoever we have for mayor, whether he be the blackest man in Philadelphia, or the worst, we would be safer under this bill than we are today."

Quay smiled appreciatively at Penrose's accurate appraisal

of the situation, promptly saw the point, and at the proper time sent word down the line that the Bullit measure must be passed. It went through in record time, and Boies Penrose's star began a rapid ascent. Quay had found not another neophyte and political washout but a partner. Whether there was ever any formal understanding between them seems not to be a matter of record, but the course of events which followed during the next two years tell the story.

The following year Quay left actual active control of much of the state political machinery in the hands of young Penrose and had himself sent to the United States Senate. From that time to the day of his death the machine's control of politics in Pennsylvania was never seriously impaired. Quay had found a worthy leader who merited a share in control and who could be trusted with it while he went on to larger spheres of action. And Penrose had found a worthy leader to follow. At no time thereafter was there any considerable friction between the two men. But they made free use of each other's selfishness.

Penrose was young, robust, and eager to learn how to make mayors, governors, senators, judges, and how to control them. Or perhaps, Presidents! He was thinking of Martin Van Buren. The State was full of interesting things to control, and Penrose was intensely interested in his own State. Not that Quay had lost interest in state affairs: far from it, but he had at last found a competent lieutenant who had understanding and ability and whom it was more dangerous to ignore than to conciliate. It was easier and more sensible to make concessions to young Penrose than to fight him, for if he were thwarted he might build a rival machine. Penrose realized all these possibilities, and he knew that Quay realized them, too, but the former realized also that Quay controlled Pennsylvania. Outside of Philadelphia. Penrose respected that pertinent fact. He respected, too, the boss's easy ability to grasp every political advantage, his withering scorn of reform and reformers, his skill and genius in actually forcing politicians and those who made them, to toe the mark—just any mark which Quay chose to name.

Although the two men had formed a working partnership which was interrupted only by Quay's death nearly twenty years later, there were fundamental differences between them which prevented a bosom companionship coming to full blossom.

First, there was the difference of birth. Quay was a son of a pious but indigent preacher. The family was of plebeian status. Preachers in those days in Pennsylvania, even the best of them, were held in low esteem and classed as harmless reformers. Their importance was acknowledged only as powerful bulwarks in shoring up the sometimes tottering economic order. Quay, to the end of his life, was conscious of and sensitive about his plebeian status. Like most minister families, poverty was their daily lot, and Matthew, as is frequently the case in such circumstances, learned to place an excessive valuation upon money. He determined to possess as much of it as he could. The manner of getting it was of little consequence compared with the absolute necessity of ridding himself of the unbearable burden of poverty. His determination to get money became stronger as the years passed, stronger than the commandments against that love of money which is the root of all evil. He early learned that politics as a fulcrum, with its ally, business, as a lever, could pry much money into his coffers. He mastered and used every means known to corrupt politics to add to his store. Franchises, contracts, appointments, tariffs, utilities—all became rich sources of supply. Quay used them all. Not only that, he used the office of state treasury as a source of private profit, for through that office alone a steady stream of from ten millions to fifteen millions of state funds annually flowed—always in one direction—increasing in later years to several times that amount.

Penrose cared nothing for money. He was a patrician by birth and as such knew the full extent of his privileges. He was as sensitive about his superior status and the proper recognition of it as was Quay about his own inferior rank. Penrose inherited wealth and there was never a minute in his life that he was really in need. Money was always to be had for the asking. As a noble patrician he possessed by divine right the machinery which made the laws to guide the unlovely rabble of plebeians and servers, and it was their lot, also by divine sanction, to scurry around and provide whatever of wealth was required to keep the noble order of life on an even keel. He, Boies Penrose, being what he was, would control legislatures, judges, and governors, while the big industries needing profits, would of course place in his hands whatever sums were necessary to maintain all that machinery of the noble order of industrialism working smoothly. But he would use none of that money for his own pleasure; he didn't need to.

Many are the stories told of Penrose's peculiar attitude towards money and towards those who were so greedy for it. He was not so good at keeping record of accounts and assets. He usually kept a roll of bills in his desk drawer and when he started out for an hour's ride or for a week's trip he would grab a hand full of bills and small change, enough to satisfy his needs, push the stuff into his pockets, and fare forth. If he ran out of money he always had credit, so why worry? He was a genius at collecting campaign funds but he never really knew at any one given time the exact standing of the exchequer, for a thousand dollar campaign contribution might be pushed into his pocket there to circulate indiscriminately with his own funds. When need arose to use the money at hand, whether for personal affairs or party affairs he threw all he had into the satisfaction of the need. For one of his position his needs were extremely simple and he never was a great spender for personal pleasures. The policies of the Republican party of which he for so long was the unquestioned czar made billions in profits for his clients, the corporations. They in turn gave him millions for party support any time he asked them to give. He used those millions, many millions, for the continuance in power of the party he loved and served, but never a cent went to enrich himself.

In Philadelphia wherever he happened to be at meal time he found an eating place and ate—and drank. If he had sufficient change to pay, all well and good; if he didn't, ditto. Present the bill some other time! And no one ever presented a bill to Boies Penrose without having it honored. Perhaps he had no recollection of incurring a debt, but he would rather pay the bill than to quibble. Once while enjoying a faultless meal with a few of the boys the proprietor came around to Boies' side apprehensively and explained to the young man that since he had eaten in there quite a few times and hadn't paid, the account was getting a little too large for comfort. In fact it amounted to considerably more than a hundred dollars.

"Oh, very well," growled the young lad, "bring on the rest of the grub here while I go and get your damned money!" So saying he lurched out of the saloon and went to a nearby bank or other source of ready cash and came back presently with the necessary amount which he placed in the hands of the smiling proprietor, then went ahead with his eating.

Years later, when he was in Washington and was leaving for Philadelphia he secured his railroad ticket but didn't offer to pay for it. The ticket agent called to him.

"Why in hell do you bother me about it?" snarled the Senator. " 'Phone my office and somebody'll bring the money."

It is little wonder, therefore, that when Penrose first entered the Legislature and became acquainted with the methods by which the masterful Quay made the wheels go round that he gave vent to his disgust at such methods in the common practice of getting money. However, since he realized that control of the machinery of politics required a great deal of money he didn't quarrel with the methods used. But this eternal snatching petty change from trusting individuals by small-time graft! Ugh! How could anyone do it and hold his self-esteem? Especially when great things were possible? The trouble was they were not big enough to grasp bigger opportunity. They had no imagination. As a matter of fact he was disgusted not so much with the methods used as with the sniveling nincompoops who had to resort to such petty rascality to hang onto the machinery.

Quay had just been delivered from one of his many narrow squeezes inherent in this brand of politics when Penrose took his first step to power. For years Quay had had his hands in the state treasurer's office, not as official secretary but as private and personal monitor to the official. When one official's term ended he saw to it that the successor was of the same mind as the previous one. The people were suspicious and at times indignant, but they always got over it. On one occasion, however, the bosses got a little careless and allowed an honest Quaker, Samuel Butler, to be elected to fill that important office. Mr. Butler, being both honest and suspicious, demanded an official balancing of the books before he took charge of the treasurer's office. Such a procedure was unheard of among politicians. The demand was so sudden and unexpected that the old gang didn't have time to return all the money they had "borrowed," and a shortage of $260,000 was revealed. Quay was frantic. He set about raising the money but was able to collect only a little more than half the amount. At the last moment his good friend, Senator Donald Cameron, remembering many good turns Quay had done for him and his father in the past, paid the remainder, thus keeping several first class Republicans out of the penitentiary. Quay blamed the bungling of the state cashier for the mixup and decided that henceforth he would go it alone. Thereupon he had himself elected to the office of state treasurer. But the state cashier, T. Blake Walters, felt differently about it and shot himself.

In 1885 Quay officially became the state treasurer but the system he had been using in conjunction with others did not change. The system was continuous and many-sided. One phase of it consisted in selecting and carefully cultivating a bank whose officers were broadminded, or timid, and making deposits of state money in said bank. A day or two later Quay, or one of the boys of the inner circle, would go down to the bank and borrow on his own unsecured note an amount almost equal to the sum previously deposited. The bank would be holding state funds on which it paid no interest, and the political borrower would be holding the bank's funds on which likewise no interest was paid. Frequently the loan to the politician was never repaid, in which case the bank failed, and the president or cashier, or both, jumped into the nearest lake or river.

After becoming state treasurer Quay deposited the sum of $400,000 of state funds in the People's Bank of Philadelphia, a set-up bank by and for politicians. Immediately thereafter he borrowed a like amount from the bank and speculated in the stock of North Chicago Railroad Company. This investment turned out all right and the loan was returned, only to have the process repeated many times. Perhaps one time too much. In 1898 the bank failed and its cashier, John S. Hopkins, committed suicide.

About two hundred banks scattered over the entire state received small deposits of state funds, primarily for the psychological political effect such a deposit would have. Only a few thousands would be deposited in these institutions; they usually were not asked for loans while holding state money as security. Ordinarily there were not more than half a dozen "active banks" on the list that received heavy deposits, running from a hundred thousand dollars to three millions. Likewise these few banks made the heaviest loans to preferred politicians.

Penrose was well acquainted with various methods of manipulation but he never adopted such methods; he didn't need to. He realized that the demands of the times had changed and that the old technic would soon have to change also. In reality a new era was being ushered in; the old regime and old methods were passing. In 1885 George B. McClellan died; in 1886 died Grant, Arthur, W. S. Hancock, Horatio Seymour, and Samuel J. Tilden. The echoes of Reconstruction were dying, and the rancid odors of the "stolen" election of 1876 were becoming very faint. The methods of Tweed, the Whiskey Ring, the Belknap scandal, the Post Star Route frauds, and the Credit Mobilier, were beginning to appear a little crude and old-fashioned. But they were still the methods of Quay. Penrose protested. Couldn't he see that they were out of date? Of course Matthew Quay could see nothing of the sort. Penrose chided him some more. Couldn't Quay and all the gang see that times had changed and with them styles in political chicanery? Not that old methods should be abandoned. Oh no! But add improvements here and there, and perhaps a new coat of paint. Go after bigger game with less risk and leave all this petty stuff to underlings. Smart politics required smart politicians!

What young Penrose was trying to convey to the alert Quay, and with a good deal more success than the latter was willing to admit, was that politics was becoming industrialized.

There was need of greater centralization in control. He saw more clearly than did the older man that these new and growing industries would demand more and more of government. And they would get it. Who, in such circumstances, was better fitted to talk to the big industrial boss than the big political boss. Then, whatever the agreement between them, make the ward-heelers and the little vote scavengers make good the agreement. He expressed something of the same philosophy years later when scandals surrounding the construction of the new State Capitol were being aired. In this conversation with Iz Durham, as reported by Walter Davenport, he said:

"Iz, practically anyone can pick pockets with a little practice. All you need is a good location, long fingers, and the soul of an ostracized rat. But it takes a pretty good man to make people step up and hand him their money hoping he'll do something for them with it. Now, about this State Capitol trouble. Iz, it's only the pickpocket politician who would go in for things like that. They make a living while nobody's looking and because nobody's looking. A long time ago I decided I didn't want that kind of money. It screams too loud when grasped. I decided to get far enough along to be able to control legislation that meant something to men with real money and let them foot the bills. Never commit yourself but always be in a position where you can if you choose. The men with money will look you up then and you don't have to worry about campaign expenses."

The Standard Oil Trust was organized in 1882. John D. Rockefeller, his brother William Rockefeller, John D. Archbold, and H. M. Flagler controlled 90% of the petroleum industry and nearly all the pipe lines of the United States. They commanded millions of dollars. Naturally they would need government help and protection. They would pay handsomely for such service. Why not abandon lesser graft to the smaller fry?

The first Bessemer converter was built in 1873. Although there was an orgy of railroad building between 1869 and 1873 most of the rails were imported. After that the steel industry of the United States really began its development in earnest. Big Business didn't become big till after 1875, then the states began to give serious attention to liberal laws which would give to industrial corporations very wide powers with a minimum of supervision.

"Take it from me, Mr. Quay, this petty thievery won't pay. You almost went to the pen for a measly hundred thousand. Don't forget that!"

"I'm still at large," replied Quay.

"Some day you'll be calling me to help you out," grunted Penrose in disgust. "Look at all the things these corporations can do; all the millions they can uncover, with a little encouragement from legislatures. And they pay well for such encouragement. Damned well!"

The Union Pacific, just then much in the public press, was a case in point. Mr. Huntington, President of the Union Pacific, admitted under oath that his company, between 1874 and 1885, had spent more than $6,000,000 for "legal" and "miscellaneous" purposes. His agent, Flanchott, at Washington, was paid $20,000 a year for his own services in "explaining things" to public servants. In fact he "may have been given" as high as $30,000 or $40,000 a year for which no vouchers were asked or given.

"But, then, public servants need an awful lot of things explained," commented Penrose doggedly.

"So does the sovereign voter," replied Mr. Quay, with a merry twinkle of the eyes.

"Sovereign voter! Bah!"

Penrose took second place to no one in his contempt for an electorate that certainly must have known what was going on but was too indifferent to fight. He was not alone in his contempt. Big Business had a like contempt not only for the voters but for the unintelligent gentry who were sent to legislatures. Most of them were downright stupid about the important things they were supposed to legislate about and were either swayed by the use of a little money or hoodwinked by the more intelligent lobbyists who were experts surrounded entirely by ignorance.

Pennsylvania is a state of large corporations. Office in any one of them is far more attractive and remunerative than the political offices. Such was the case forty years ago. Such is the case today. The President of the Pennsylvania Railroad Company, for example, was paid at that time a salary of $50,-000 a year; the Governor of the State was paid $10,000 a year. The former controlled 150,000 employees; the latter not more than 500. The presidency of the railroad lasts for life; the Governor's term is a hectic and uncertain four years. There are in the Pennsylvania Railroad system, or were then, nearly three hundred executives who had more pay, more power, and more authority than the Governor of the State; and there were several dozen corporations in the State only a little less imposing than the above mentioned railroad. It can't be a matter of wonder, therefore, that for years in Pennsylvania, as well as in many other states, the best of the annual crop of young men were absorbed by the corporations, leaving politics to absorb the less capable, the less intelligent, and the less moral.

To this general rule Boies Penrose was a notable and refreshing exception. And that explains much. He was of giant intellect, though so much cannot be said for his morals. His superior intellect and social background could have been counted on to have placed him in the foremost rank in the industrial world or among the professions, had it not been for his monumental sloth. He was heroically and magnificently lazy. The difference between him and the other politicians was that the latter were greedy, stupid, and without morals, while the former was without greed, without morals, and without stupidity. It was much easier for him to be leader in this gang than in the more alert and highly competitive business world. Therefore he chose the road to leadership that required the least possible amount of exertion. And political leadership had glamour and prestige and power of directing policies for millions and received their homage. People pointed him out wherever he went. He possessed no ethical standards to bother him. He could tolerate their greed without participating in its fruit; he could enjoy their lustful and shameless conduct without repeating their cringing apologies or adopting their hypocritical furtiveness.

But his greatest pleasure was the recreation he derived from riding his favorite horse out into the country about Harrisburg. He owned the best riding horses to be had, which he kept in a barn near the capitol under the care of a trusted Negro groom. The longer he stayed in Harrisburg the more frequently he made long excursions about the countryside in order to be free from the stews of the city. More important, however, he wanted to study the many types of birds and trees. Fishing, as a sport, didn't appeal to him. Small game hunting was not especially enticing, but searching out new species of plant life, recognizing by their botanical names all the trees, and learning the call note of birds, thrilled him and drew him back to their haunts time and again.

Penrose was distinctly a product of his times. However, if that statement should remain unmodified one would get only a partial and incorrect picture of the man. Not only was he a product of his period but in some degree the moulder of it. He was a thorough student of politics and all its varied manifestations. In his early Harvard days he became an avid reader and the habit continued with him. Certainly the great panorama of new forces stirring to national life all about him during his 'teens and twenties held a profound interest for him. The first glorious bursting of bonds after the "peace" of 1865 meant for the victors an unbridled orgy of wealth-getting. It produced the first crop of the newly rich which promptly put forward its claims of social equality. They challenged the envied heights of social favor held by the old aristocracy of gentle breeding, a class in America which was being rapidly submerged. In Philadelphia this had some curious effects.

Immediately after the war wealth came suddenly, and in large measure, to a class of industrialists who had never been accustomed to more than comfortable subsistence. Many of them were entirely innocent of any culture, but they and their large brood of children plunged into a lavish display of extravagance, jewels and gowns, in an effort to outdo the hospitality and social gyrations of the cultured families of the city. One of the leading jewelers of the times said that due to the inflation of the post-war days (Civil War) there were more precious stones and costly jewels sold than in the previous forty years of his business career. The demand for diamonds at any price was so great that it was difficult to fill orders, and he added that the peculiar feature about the trade was that a vast majority of his increased list of customers were entirely unknown to him. One gaudily dressed lady entered his store, purchased a $5000 necklace, paid for it, coolly fastened it about her neck, and wore it on her way home. A regular reign of shoddy and vulgar display dominated the city. Whether in church, in theaters, or at social functions, a profusion of diamonds flashed from hands that had known nothing but drudgery. So ostentatious was the display of fine stones on any and every occasion that the vulgarity of it became a little tiresome. All the women of culture, in order to be different and mask a rebuke, absolutely abandoned the use of jewels. Entertainments and social affairs soon became crowded with these new aristocrats of wealth whose expenditures were so lavish and gaudy that the better element could no longer keep pace with them. The entire social world of the city became so unsettled that the former leaders had to withdraw and form the exclusive Saturday Evening Club, to which Sarah Boies Penrose belonged, with strict rules against extravagance and display.

When the prosperity bubble collapsed in 1873, this display and extravagance was speedily checked and within a short time the pawnbroker liquidated the last of the precious stones.

The panic of 1873 lasted five years and shook the business world from top to bottom. More than 40% of the railway mileage of the entire country went into bankruptcy. By 1877 there were 47,000 business failures in the United States with a loss much greater than the total indemnity which France paid to Germany. In order to be protected from such far-reaching effects of any similar panic in the future, a new type of business organization developed, and as usual Pennsylvania took the initiative by passing at the beginning of the panic in 1874, a law which provided that companies be incorporated with more strictly limited liabilities for stockholders and investors. Thus a large degree of protection was drawn from the investor and given to the promoter. When Penrose came to power he turned thumbs down on every attempt to modify this law. Years later a man by the name of Insull profited enormously by that type of law.

The panic of 1873–1878 ended the first great wave of profiteering and lavish spending only to be succeeded in a few years by an undreamed of rush into another period of exploitation and spoliation that continued almost uninterrupted for a full generation. And in one respect the years which followed were the exact duplicates of the years which have followed in the wake of every depression in America—much greater concentration of wealth in fewer hands, enlargement of the dependent class, decrease in the margin of safety for the masses, and a more rigid control of the machinery of government by the feudal lords of wealth. Penrose argued that these leaders of industry were entitled to every protection and encouragement the state could give. Didn't they furnish steady work to the mass of workers? And didn't they furnish money for taxes? Didn't they make the nation great? The era of corporate business and corporate politics had come. That meant greater concentration of privilege and political power.

Boies Penrose was prepared to take the lead in this even closer relationship between business and politics. No man in the country knew more thoroughly the needs of each and was listened to with greater confidence than he. He was President of the Pennsylvania Senate two terms, 1889–91 and threw his influence to every measure looking to greater freedom for industry. The direction of his influence took almost always the direction legislation took. In this new industrial period statecraft became less obvious in its methods. Lawyers, plain and fancy, crowded into politics and blurred the hitherto simple picture. Being possessed of a certain leisure for party affairs and accustomed to rendering "opinions," and being apt in arguing both sides of all questions, they were preferred as candidates for office. Their talents were especially attractive to captains of industry, for the law being used by many as the profession of adroit deceit, they could readily conceal the purpose of business in politics. Throughout this whole period of

IN A PLAYFUL MOOD
During a visit to a Florida Grapefruit grove

SENATOR PENROSE AT THE WHEEL OF HIS YACHT "BETTY"

acquisitive politics it has been the lawyer, with his special code of ethics, who has played the leading, if frequently ignoble, role in the political forum. The political lawyer soon became the corporation attorney, and the corporation attorney soon became Congressman and Senator and lobbyist with his major purpose that of favoring all proposals that favored the industrial boss and of defeating every measure inimical to him.

"Thereupon," says Beard, "the substance of politics became too elusive for the eye of the inexperienced; what was going on behind the scenes was seldom fully known to the audience. For instance, until a scandal exploded the inner works, it was not disclosed that several powerful members of Congress who spoke so earnestly on the urgent necessity for progress in the Far West during the sixties had handsome gifts of Union Pacific or Credit Mobilier securities safely laid away. To use a later illustration, until the agents of William Randolph Hearst purloined the papers in the case, the great American electorate was unaware that the Honorable Joseph B. Foraker of Ohio, who represented that state in the Senate and who wrote the anti-Trust plank for the Republican platform of 1900, had received generous retainers from the Standard Oil interests. Neither did that electorate know that the Senator had received, while in office, a large sum from the same source to purchase a Republican newspaper."

Penrose was thoroughly versed in the methods of such control and coloring of public opinion, of drawing the curtain at the appropriate time to reveal only such parts of the act as it was wise for the public to see. He realized before any of the accepted leaders of his party that the years just ahead were to constitute the "utility age"; that every company had to use public property for private gain. He knew also that the trend was distinctly toward consolidation of ownership and that political control of the privileges to be granted to corporations would have to continue its concentration of control and increase it.

"And why not?" he asked of a critic of the times. "All these riches and opportunities were put here to use, weren't they? Who's going to develop them if we leaders don't? Of course there's a little graft here and there. Try and stop it! But, hell! We can't sit down and be good while we starve to death." In fact the rush toward consolidation was already upon them.

In 1882 the United Gas and Improvement Company was organized in Philadelphia, destined later to become one of America's foremost utilities. There was very little attempt at regulation of corporations in Penrose's day, and such restraining clauses as were incorporated in franchises were usually ignored. Syndicates were formed to exploit public utilities, corporations being formed for building, equipping, combining, and unifying water, light, and transportation facilities. Soon the street railways and lighting companies of New York, Philadelphia, Chicago, and Pittsburg, as well as all the utilities of a public nature in most of the smaller towns and cities of New York, Pennsylvania, Connecticut, Rhode Island, Massachusetts, Ohio, Indiana, Georgia, Mississippi, New Hampshire, and Maine, were in the hands of six men—C. T. Yerkes, P. A. B. Widener, W. L. Elkins, W. C. Whitney, Thomas F. Ryan, and John Dolan. In 1873 when the panic struck most of them down, there were more than 2000 railroad and transportation companies in the United States. In the eighties this number was reduced to a few dozen. In 1870 New York City had more than thirty street railroad companies whose lines consisted of bobtailed cars run by horses and mules, lighted by oil lamps and other similar old-fashioned appliances. All this was changed in the eighties when corporate management brought all main lines under one head. With the advent of electric power an era of municipal public improvements was inaugurated and New York was soon supplied with electric lights, telephones, electric street-railways, and other modern conveniences—all controlled by a half-dozen corporations. The trolleys and lights of all New Jersey soon were in the hands of a single corporation, the Public Service Corporation of New Jersey. All these corporations and the bosses who ran them soon came to be the most powerful clients the United States Senators had.

In the eighties and nineties the men who were developing public utilities were at the same time in control of municipal politics. Thomas F. Ryan and William C. Whitney, through Tammany Hall, controlled New York City; Charles T. Yerkes was the absolute boss of Chicago's mayor and aldermen; P. A. B. Widener and W. L. Elkins ran the City Hall in Philadelphia, as an integral part of the Quay machine, and through that machine connection had a dominant influence throughout the state. Penrose unified that control and brought every ounce of its political influence into his own hands. Mark Hanna not only bossed the Cleveland street railways but was the Republican boss of Ohio; Roswell Flower, boss of the Brooklin Rapid Transit Company, was at the same time governor of New York; and Patrick Calhoun was the boss of utilities of San Francisco and boss of its government as well. The Public Service Corporation of New Jersey was very active in all state and local politics, for only through politics could franchises be obtained which would enable corporations to "serve" the public. Politicians went after public franchises with a special degree of fondness and spent whatever amount of money was necessary to secure them. The politician was usually a lawyer of sufficient skill to write the franchise to favor the corporation instead of the public.

Penrose early determined to be in a position to dictate the

terms and prices of franchises, especially for his own beloved Philadelphia. His greatest and perhaps only real ambition was to serve his city as its mayor, but it was only after his defeat for that honor that he turned his attention to national politics. For the present he was very well satisfied to turn his attention to city and state affairs and let Quay go on to Washington.

In assuming state control of politics in Pennsylvania Penrose was laboring under no rosy illusions as to the type of control that was necessary. When he first went to Harrisburg he was the youngest member of the Legislature, the largest on the hoof, and very soon the most popular. After one year in the House he was elected to the Senate, being at the time only a few days within the legal age limit. For eleven years he represented the Sixth District in Philadelphia, the richest district in the state. During these twelve years at the Capital he was the politician superb. And during all that time he never rose above the status of a rather cheap politician, but much above it in understanding. Never cared to do more. He knew what politics demanded and willingly met those demands. Some apologists for him have tried to make it appear that during his first years in politics he followed the star of idealism. Such, however, doesn't seem to be borne out by the facts. From the very beginning he followed whatever course best suited his pleasure and purpose. By way of introducing himself to politics and getting the feel of the game he had championed a reform candidate, Mr. Jayne. Incidentally he was able to demonstrate to the gang that he knew how to play their game and that in the future they might as well keep him in mind. He championed a reform charter for Philadelphia, to be sure, but merely to make it easier to control the power at the head of things. He was very far-sighted in all such things.

The story of how Penrose built up and consolidated his control over Pennsylvania politics is a familiar one to many persons, and a very interesting one. It began, of course, when he first went to Harrisburg and was a continuing process, but he really never got into the matter of mastering the technic till Quay went to the United States Senate. Along about 1890 Penrose made his first comprehensive tour of the state. Many others followed in the years after that.

There were at that time about 5000 election districts in the state and about 25,000 active party workers, members of the Republican Organization. He wanted to meet these workers personally, especially in the strategic centers. He visited every one of the 67 counties, and in some of them he spent enough time to "look about a little," to meet all the committeemen and to talk over every detail of their work. Of course the committeemen and workers were anxious to meet Senator Penrose, the Big Leader from Philadelphia. That was before the automobile and good roads, and life was less cosmopolitan than it is today. It was more community-conscious. Distinguished people seldom visited small, out-of-the-way places; their voices and names were not made familiar by the radio; their pictures and doings were not publicized by the news reel. Metropolitan newspapers circulated only sparingly beyond a city's limits. The visit of a state senatorial leader was an event. Especially so since Quay was a household word all over the state and Penrose was associated with him.

In every community Penrose had many invitations to stay with this committeeman or that leader, or the mayor, etc., but he refused them all, for to show favoritism to any one in a community would inevitably cause jealousy and lose a vote. He made it a rule always to stay at a hotel and invite the various officials and friends to meet him there. Frequently dinner for all—at his expense.

"Any Democrats present?" he always asked, by way of beginning. That never failed to bring his guests around to a good laugh, or perhaps just a pleasant smile, but it introduced his subject. The Great Republican Party was his theme at every gathering and he followed it with gusto.

"We do things for you. Business is good. . . . Coal miners work and draw wages because there's a market for the coal. . . . The great manufacturing concerns of the state use the raw materials from all over the state and put thousands to work at good wages. Who finds them markets for their products? Who maintains profits for them so they can employ you? Who keeps up the glorious tariff? Who keeps out cheap labor? When you need better roads, a bridge across the river, better schools, more work who provides them for you? . . . We look after all these things for you down at Harrisburg. We do this by keeping all the machinery of government working smoothly, but we can't do it unless you supply us with good Representatives and Senators who know how to co-operate with the leaders. I'd rather have a good Democrat than a poor Republican. Yes, sir! Our party depends on your support. . . ."

He never failed to visit the local newspapers and make friends with the local editor. Printing contracts, an occasional job for a doubtful leader, cajolery, and many devices were used to keep the local press boosting the type of candidate who would follow the leaders. In a campaign money from state headquarters was always to be had provided it could be used to elect friendly candidates. If an independent lawmaker went to Harrisburg who refused to follow the leaders he was denied the help of the state and local Organization for re-election and he was retired to private life.

If—and it's a very large if—the program of reform had offered any hope of success and stability there is no doubt that Penrose would have insinuated himself into that movement, but since for years past every effort of the reformers and social uplifters had ended in such pitiable spectacles of ineptitude his contempt for them knew no bounds. When one observes the puny results of reform in Pennsylvania in the last half of the last century one is inclined to respect Penrose for his scorn. Look briefly at the record!

In 1839 Simon Cameron was appointed chairman of a commission of two men to convey for the War Department the sum of $100,000 in gold to Prairie Du Chien on the Mississippi where it was to be given, in accordance with a treaty sponsored by the War Department, to the Winnebago Indians. Sadly enough the Indians never saw the gold. This was in the days of the "Pet Banks" of the Jacksonian democracy, and Cameron was owner and proprietor of one such bank at Middletown. The laws were quite liberal about the issuance of money by these banks. By 1863 there were more than twelve thousand kinds of money afloat in the United States, some of it counterfeit, each kind good in the locality of its issuance but the value thereof depreciating in the ratio of its distance from home. Prairie Du Chien was a long way from Middletown and the Cameron bank's money was without value to the Indians, nevertheless, Cameron deposited the hundred thousand in gold in his bank and delivered to the Indians a like amount of his own bank's money. Worthless! Of course there was a scandal and a lot of noise. The Government set aside Cameron's commission, but that was a matter of no embarrassment to him. He was denounced in Congress as a swindler of "the poor Indians," but he kept right on being a good Democrat—for a while. Then he turned Whig, later honoring the Republicans by joining them.

In 1845 he took James Buchanan's place in the United States Senate.

In 1857 he again had himself elected to the United States

Senate by the simple method of bribery. By this time he was an excellent Republican. The Democrats had a majority in the Legislature of Pennsylvania, but the time had come to "run them out of power." So, the Republican machine was geared to accomplish this objective. Charles Bingham Penrose, grandfather of Boies, was a leading member of the state senate. When it became quite clear that Republican Cameron couldn't obtain a majority over John Forney, Democrat, in their struggle to be elected to the United States Senate, Penrose caused the session to be adjourned till the following day. When, on the morrow the Democratic majority met in high glee to proclaim the victory of their candidate, they soon were thrown into high dudgeon, for when the vote was taken Cameron had a majority of one vote. Overnight three Democrats had accepted bribes to vote for Cameron; Grandfather Penrose had seen to that. Patriotic ire became so active and intense in the environs of the Pennsylvania capital that not a hotel in the city would allow the three vote-sellers to cross the threshold and they immediately departed for parts unknown—in search of balmier temperatures. Their sin was a grievous one, not for accepting a bribe, but for accepting it from the wrong party. Yet, Simon Cameron, the bribe-giver, went to the United States Senate full of honor.

Three years later this same Simon Cameron, happy swindler of the Winnebago, successful briber of people's representative, and political boss extraordinary of Pennsylvania, so dominated that state's delegation in the National Republican Convention in Chicago that he received the delegation's solid "favorite son" vote for nomination to the Presidency in opposition to Honest Abe Lincoln. And so powerful was his influence that Lincoln had to place him in his Cabinet as Secretary of War. As a matter of fact Cameron had demanded the cabinet post of Secretary of the Treasury, and was on the point of receiving it when such a storm of protest and abuse swirled about Lincoln and his advisers that the appointment was changed to read: Simon Cameron, Secretary of War. In less than ninety days after the war began we find a Congressional Committee (July, 1861) investigating Cameron and the unbearable stench coming from the War Department, and issuing a scathing rebuke of his administration of that Department. Cameron quit the Cabinet a little later, on request of the President, and was appointed Minister to Russia. He soon tired of Russia, however, and had himself elected again to the United States Senate— by the usual methods.

In this election bribery was a little more open and powerful. The sum of $20,000 was offered one member of the Legislature, Dr. T. J. Boyer, for his vote. In a few months we see the state Legislature putting on the robe of righteousness and instructing the Attorney-General to start criminal proceedings. Curiously enough the prosecution soon fizzled out.

In 1868 the same story. Twenty-one Republicans, enough to hold the balance of power, pledged themselves not to vote for Cameron. And they held out—till the ante was raised, but Cameron was elected, as usual.

At the end of his term he was given another whopping reelection, only to resign in 1877, forcing the election of his son, Donald, to fill his place. This last transaction was a little more difficult than the others. In fact the honor of working for the people was getting more complicated and expensive all the time. Twenty-seven stalwart Republicans rebelled in caucus and refused to vote for the son, Donald. Thereupon the Legislature was speedily adjourned and the members allowed to go to their homes for some rest; they had been tired out by their arduous labors. In the quiet of their homes the Cameron henchmen went to work on the rebels individually with the result that all but five capitulated, and son, Donald, went to the

United States Senate. There he remained till 1897 when Boies Penrose replaced him.

Simon Cameron served longer in the Senate than any other man in the history of the country but he left not a single speech in its records. About all that remains to posterity of his political philosophy is his definition of a good politician: "An honest politician is one who, when he is bought, stays bought."

Boies Penrose was thoroughly conversant with the black record of the elder Cameron and all the vile methods employed consistently to give triumph to boodle politics. He had seen "the inside of the works," which time and again gave victory to blustering, grafting, and criminal politicians; knew of Kemble and his shameless "addition, division, and silence"; saw Quay plunder bank after bank which carried deposits of state funds—and the resultant suicides; saw convictions and confession of criminal guilt of high politicians who, before reaching the penitentiary, were handed pardons "with the compliments of the state government." He saw, furthermore, wave after wave of reform agitation lash itself into white fury only to spend its force without ever reaching shore; saw reformer after reformer rush against the bulwarks of boodle only to be smashed beyond recognition. Smashed mainly because of their own stupidity or that of the public. And year after year the same dear apathetic public re-elected these same swindlers, bribers, treasury-raiders, and petty thieves to higher office! No wonder he sniffed a little disdainfully and marked up the total results of all such efforts at uplift at exactly zero. No wonder he accepted and acted upon Israel Durham's political code: "The men we nominate must be the men we can control." The reform group could seldom control or depend on their nominees or their leaders, for there was no cohesive element to hold such groups together from one election to another.

In trying to answer the puzzling question of why Pennsylvania, particularly Philadelphia, has displayed for generations such an astoundingly corrupt and putrid a brand of politics, one recalls Heine's famous phrase, "We do not take possession of our ideas but are possessed by them." In seeking to understand why a group of citizens perhaps above the average level in morality, virtue, and general goodness, and with a high regard for the proprieties of religion, should allow themselves to be robbed year after year, systematically and thoroughly without an effective protest, one must realize how absolute the tyranny of concepts can be. Penrose and his intelligent lieutenants understood it well and profited greatly thereby. Many of us are so chained to the past, we have such reverence for obedience to established custom and law that we resent and sternly repress all variability and all tendency to change. When society becomes so congealed—and all societies become progressively so with age—by what Walter Bagehot called the "cake of custom," that it cannot or will not break the crust, adopt new attitudes, change old to new, it becomes impossible to make progress.

About 1905 Philadelphia had approximately 300,000 families, not more than 20,000 of which could be classed among the congested, shiftless, slatternly, or submerged type. Thirty thousand of these families were well-to-do, some of them very wealthy, leaving the remaining 250,000 families, according to a critic of the time, more comfortably situated than any other population of equal income in the world. But their horizons were exceptionally limited and localized. They still had the old decentralized ward system of school management till 1904, and their interests and judgments seemed never to transcend the ward boundary lines. Philadelphia was a wilderness of small homes in which a man kept his reputation unspotted in his own ward independent of what he did at City Hall or in the market place. Sam Ashbridge, who was Mayor from 1899 to 1903, and who reeked in graft, bribery, and license, said that he had laid the foundations for his campaigns and his political power by speaking frequently before Sunday school groups, local church clubs, and the like. But during his Administration Philadelphia paid $2.64 a ton for garbage disposal while Boston was getting a similar service for only 63¢ a ton. The highest bidder instead of the lowest was given the contract only after the latter had been hounded out of the city by the police.

If a policeman stole money he was lenient in other matters, too, and went to church regularly. Policemen, born in the neighborhood of their daily activities, protected dives, vote-stealing, and small school children with equal impartiality and efficiency. From the council everybody got something; corporations got franchises, gave bribes to politicians, and free passes to their constituents; manufacturers got the use of the streets, freedom from factory laws, and low tax valuations; respectable people were kowtowed to, got large contributions for charities, and various institutions. In a period of ten years $60,000,000 was extracted from the taxpayers and spent on city improvements. This created a steady stream of contracts to enrich leaders, good wages to workers whose jobs were secured by the ward heelers, and good profits to home manufacturers.

These things sapped the fiber of a whole people caught up in the flux of progress. Anyone who condemned any special step in this whole method of growth was not tolerated. Too close an examination of trivialities was shunned and Philadelphia literally oozed goodness and respectability. And the Philadelphia machine dominated at all times the State Organization which in turn owned the Governor and Legislature.

Philadelphia has long had perhaps an unreasonable regard for old families, old traditions and habits, and a reluctance to accept anything new merely because it is new. A native of that city for years refused to entertain for one instant any doubt that an individual who was personally honest and moral could possibly be a party, as a member of a group, to unjust measures. A group of aldermen represented law and order and it was all but sacrilege to criticize them. Especially was it true if the critic happened to be an outsider—and Pennsylvania had its share. To a true native, loyalty to tradition, to the city and its honored institutions, to neighbors, to party, was the highest possible loyalty. It blinded them to a sense of loyalty to such an abstract concept as social justice, truth, community welfare.

How else can be explained the apparent ease with which the bosses of Philadelphia and their machine could always dominate the Republican State Conventions? Representation in these conventions theoretically was on the basis of legislative apportionment according to the voting population; practically it was related to the Republican vote cast. Although the city of Philadelphia never had an honest voting population which would entitle it to a majority representation in the convention; the vote was padded regularly to the extent of twenty to thirty thousand, thus rendering helpless the minority rural delegates. The Philadelphia majority could always be swelled to meet all exigencies. In spite of this downright crookedness the best people in the city and state would vote year after year for the crooks who perpetrated these outrages against the electoral machinery. John Wanamaker, a merchant of wealth and position, who battled for clean politics in his city of Philadelphia, and for the entire state, in his tilts with Quayism and Penroseism, stoutly condemned the entire program of these unscrupulous bosses and called them all the names that could be used in polite society, but after finding himself defeated by the most open and outrageous thievery, turned about face and supported the full ticket in the election on the theory that one had to support the "regular" ticket. That meant the Republican party. It was a greater sin, according to this standard, to revolt against the rottenness of one's own party by voting "independent" than to tolerate the most vicious and scurrilous debauchery imaginable. That attitude reflected the prevailing sentiment of his city and times.

There are many reasons why in Philadelphia and the whole of Pennsylvania, the political robbers allied themselves with the Republican party. In New York it was the Democratic party. But Pennsylvania got its direction from Simon Cameron and Thaddeus Stevens during and following the Civil War. These party workers banded themselves into a severely disciplined group known as the Organization. The word came to be synonymous with dishonesty, treachery, and loot.

The Organization roughly was composed of three groups. First, there was the small group of party officials,—insiders,— who formulated policies and developed strategy, chief lieutenants over districts or cities, precinct and ward captains, and petty heelers. It was a compact and dependable group. From the lowest precinct private to the top boss every one had his definite duty to perform in seeing the voters, conducting elections, delivering his quota of votes, etc. The personnel of the Organization usually had no other occupation: either he held a sinecure job created for the purpose, or he occupied a strategic position where he could swing valuable contracts, state printing jobs, franchises, make appointments—from all of which some considerable advantage would accrue to them. The numbers of such personnel could be expanded considerably to fit all emergencies. And woe to these party captains, generals, or privates, if the geographical divisions under them failed to register winning votes at elections.

Next came the party members who were interested only at elections and who voted according to precedent and party labels. It was the business of this Organization Personnel to keep the normal party membership constantly "sold" on the policies and candidates and achievements of the party.

Third, the ever-growing list of cynical doubters, and passive onlookers who had lost interest in politics, and who were convinced of the futility of voting. They had to be persuaded, cajoled, enticed, maybe given petty jobs, but they had to be brought to the polls somehow.

A fund of more than ten millions of dollars annually was at the disposal of the Organization to be distributed among the charities and other institutions of the State. Yet, in the hands of the Organization, not a dollar of this fund would find its way into the hands of any institution, however deserving or urgent the need, unless the officers of the institution became the avowed and public supporters of the bosses who had the power to distribute these bounties. One example is enlightening.

A well-known minister was Chairman of the Board of one of the important state charitable institutions which had been receiving annually certain sums for its current expenses. The appropriations were expected as a matter of course. The minister in question, a close observer of political morality, or the lack of it, had become outraged at the Penrose method and at Quay's manipulations and denounced such practices openly and publicly. When the time came for the institution which the minister represented to receive its appropriation of $50,000 nothing happened. Weeks kept passing regularly but no money came, and the situation was getting desperate; unless the appropriations came through the institution would have to close.

Finally the Organization sent word to the minister that upon public declaration of support of the Quay-Penrose regime the funds would be forthcoming. The minister at last had to do a humiliating about-face and publicly commend him whom he had previously condemned.

Each Legislature disbursed many millions of dollars, increasing with the years until now the sums of taxpayer dollars total around the hundred million mark, yet never a dollar was appropriated without first ascertaining that the project receiving a share of this fund was administered by a friend of the Organization.

The Organization owned in absolute fee simple every office holder, big, little, medium, or substitute, in every city and county in the State. In Philadelphia alone there were in excess of ten thousand such "servants." Every mayor was a tool, policemen were not only detectives to watch good citizens and "meddlers," but their chief duties were to protect the pools of vice and gambling so the bosses might draw from them an uninterrupted stream of tribute. Those who refused to be shaken down were raided and padlocked. At the election places the chief duties of policemen were to secure and protect all ballot boxes against a "recount."

In the larger cities the bosses forced all public utilities to join them by giving valuable franchises only to those who, as old Simon Cameron years earlier expressed it, "when they were bought would stay bought." Fabulous millions which these Public Service Corporations were to extract from the public, were given away in many cases to the utility companies without a thin dime's compensation to the State. But these same companies gave tidy sums yearly to the bosses. And in the list of heavy stockholders in said companies were to be found many veteran members of the political Organization. One such company with a stock valuation of six millions revealed that the affable Izzy Durham, valiant cohort and lieutenant of Boies Penrose, controlled a majority of the stock.

It isn't surprising to learn that as Big Business, corporate business, needed favors at the hands of the legislature, it sent its purchasing agent to the source of favors, plentifully supplied with cash and hokum, and proceeded to buy in the open market all the favors in sight. But with several hundred corporations seeking favors at the same source competition became very expensive as well as bitter and noisy. Penrose sent the lobbyists home and devised a better method of contact. It was better for his bossism and of more value to the corporations to deal directly through him for such concessions as they wanted. He exacted flat sums from the corporations in turn for promises given them that no legislation antagonistic to a given concern would pass or remain in force. Thus nearly every corporate business in the state found it desirable to fall in line, depending on the favors wanted, of course, and make its donations to headquarters. The Organization expected and obtained an annual average sum of approximately one hundred thousand dollars.

In addition to the above amounts in off years, swollen to fit emergencies, there must be added even larger amounts from the army of cohorts of the machine and salaried employees of the city. The grand total of political assessments from city employees in the ten-year period from 1903–12 amounted to $4,098,368. There was a regular schedule of forced donations from all salaried employees of the city ranging from 3% for salaries of $600 to $1200, to 12% for those of $10,000 and above. We must add to this, donations from keepers of saloons, brothels, and all the dives and gambling dens needing protection. Adding another column we find contractors, sub-contractors, city laborers, Public Service Corporations, forming altogether an army of about 30,000 in Philadelphia alone, plac-

ing into the Organization's strong box more millions and into
the Organization's ballot boxes probably an irreducible minimum of 100,000 votes on election days.

Penrose preferred smart politics played in deadly earnest.
He found that type only in the closely knit groups that had
enormous stakes to win.

The long list of boodle triumphs, one following closely
upon another, had the effect of progressive applications of
anaesthetics which slowly but surely deaden sensitivity. Their
continued success seemed, in the estimation of at least a part
of the public, to justify the unscrupulousness of their methods
and to gild the unworthiness of their aims. There was a certain
magnificence and glamour in the untiring virility with which
they pursued, captured, and devoured every morsel of office,
honor and emolument in sight. Their piracy, like that of the
Vikings, lost its vulgarity in its successful audacity and in the
sense of futility and contempt awakened by the feebleness of
public resistance. What they did was necessary politics according to their code and public affairs could be conducted in no
better way.

The public came firmly to believe that the affairs of office
could be successfully conducted only with a little accompany-
ing graft and the usual spoils. They were willing to accept
Izzy Durham's "machine code" at its face value. The following is a part of a speech made by one of Durham's key men in
a city campaign:

"The cohesive power of the 'machine' is the offices. There
are ten thousand of them at the disposal of the Organization
(in Philadelphia.) The Poles, Hungarians, Italians, and the
other foreigners who come here vote with us because we control the offices. They want favors and know they cannot get

them unless they vote with us. In New York they vote with Tammany for the same reason.

"It is not a question of —— or any other man. If the Organization does not control the offices it cannot maintain its strength; and if it has not power how is it going to reward those who are faithful to it? But it is powerful now, and under this administration no man can hope for office unless he is true to the Organization.

"The ticket nominated is the ticket of the Organization. You are a part of the Organization, and if you do not stand by it, how can you expect it to stand by you? The Organization is strong because it controls the offices which control all the contributions that go to make it strong. Without the offices this great organization would crumble and fall. It voted today $40,000 to buy 80,000 tax receipts to qualify 80,000 voters. This money came from the office-holders. Without the offices who would do the work in your wards and divisions?"

Penrose, first, last, and all the time, was an Organization man. But being an organization man didn't mean necessarily that he accepted slavishly all their methods and devices. Astute politician that he was he realized that it was necessary to have support and power at hand when he needed it, at the same time not allowing others to know how much of either he commanded. Instead of becoming a worker in the ranks and ascending the ladder from the bottom he elected to begin at the top and let his power and influence trickle downward.

He had crashed the gates of party power when he forced the election, in defiance of the local bosses in his own bailiwick, of a reform ticket. That was an insolent thing to undertake, especially by a stripling just out of college and an impressive member of the unapproachable aristocracy of America's most aristocratic, complacent, and wicked city. But his insolence and cool courage produced a dazzling victory. Nothing succeeds like success—especially in terms of politics. The political world embraced him as a long lost brother.

Quay, Penrose knew, had never been in full command of Philadelphia politics, though he had desperately wanted that control, so Penrose played one rival faction against another to gain the great Mr. Quay's favor and support. That was shrewd politics and Quay was the first to recognize it as such. Having been elected to the Legislature he began at once and in his own way courting the favor of the Master. He soon convinced Quay that it would be good policy to change certain tactics, such for example as supporting a lot of unimportant bosses in Philadelphia who had been opposing a new charter for the city. Quay, sensing at last the presence of a powerful young aid whose help might be the deciding factor in bringing the City of Brotherly Love under the Quay banner, gave the word to his well-trained legislative puppets and they jumped to instant obedience by voting rousing approval of the very measure they had previously so ardently defeated. Thus Penrose enhanced his prestige enormously in Philadelphia, in turn threw its benefits to the Boss, who in turn divided responsibility with Penrose.

The next step was to help Quay realize his ambition to go to the United States Senate. That was not going to be an easy task. If left to the free and intelligent choice of the people of Pennsylvania Quay could not have polled one vote in ten in the entire State. But the vote in Pennsylvania, or any other portion of the nation, was seldom untrammelled or intelligent. Penrose gladly aided in having Quay elected, for at one stroke he could win his gratitude and gain greater freedom in state affairs.

The election in 1887 which sent Matthew Stanley Quay to Washington was not greatly different from dozens of other elections in the heyday of the Cameronian dynasty. Popular election of United States Senators had not yet been invented and the field of operations was quite circumscribed. All one had to do was to concentrate on a few dozen or so legislators, having liberal allowances of cash, of course, and convince them of their patriotic duty. A rough division of the personnel of the legislative body gives some notion of the problem of the bosses in electing their man to the high office of United States Senator. The Republicans rated from 70% up to 85% of the membership from year to year. A minority, and at times a very small minority in both parties, were honest, high-minded gentlemen who knew what was best in the matter both of legislation and representation, and they could be counted on to stand for high principles. But a majority in both parties could be and frequently were bought or swayed by the use of money or promises of jobs or contracts for friends. The only question which most of them had to contend with, therefore, was to determine which candidate or policy would pay most in coin of the realm or in valuable concessions. However, the bosses of the legislatures have always understood that condition and have been adroit in finding in short order the most vulnerable link in most politicians' armor. In this Penrose was adept.

When, therefore, Quay determined to go to the United States Senate, Penrose took the reins in his own hands and began casually toppling the violent and vociferous opposition. At this time Penrose was immensely popular among the legislators. He was the noble patrician of honorable lineage and aristocratic connections. His forbears had created the Commonwealth. In appearance he was every inch the majestic representative of an historic past. The vast majority of the remaining group were just the common run-of-the-mine lot. They recognized their plebeian status. But for the Prince to step into their rather crude pleasures and actually demonstrate how lovely it was to be of such easy morals and to adopt such plebeian tastes it pleased their democratic instincts mightily. He had not yet created such unsavory gossip about his escapades and sometimes lurid orgies. And in his first attempt at mass bludgeoning there was clearly demonstrated the differences in method between the two men. Quay as leader of the Republican party compelled his followers to stay in line by the liberal use of fear; Penrose appealed to their self-interest. It may be repeated here that frequently the cheap, vulgar, or servile type of legislator was elected in the first place. It was one of the principal functions of the machine to head off at the source the attempt of any independent candidate or public-spirited citizen to get into office. In a great majority of cases this attempt was successful. It was particularly true of state and national congresses where independence, once in office would prove too embarrassing for the machine.

Quay kept an elaborate index system, constantly revised and kept up-to-date, where he could at a moment's notice give full and complete data on a man's sins. An important function in this connection was to make any activity of uprightness and independence appear, by garbling a report of it, as sin in the minds of the average voter. When, therefore, any person in any part of the state, be he Democrat or Republican, decided to move into public life, Quay knew almost instantly how to encourage him or head him back to private life. Henchmen of the machine combed the man's record and private life from the birth of the man's grandfather down to the present to discover and record any shady practice or occupation, or any unorthodox religious and political views, which might be turned against him or his family. These henchmen of the machine included policemen, newspaper reporters, ward-heelers, and an assortment of hangers-on who hoped for some nod of recognition from the Great One himself. And most of the information was astonishingly correct, at least in its implication of some unsavory action which the unhappy victim preferred to have remain a secret.

Thus once when Quay was battling to put as much distance as possible between himself and prison, a Democratic member of the Legislature was becoming very bold about what he was going to do to the dear Mr. Quay till the latter merely confronted him with some information.

"Better not take this matter too seriously, my friend," admonished the undisturbed Quay, "or you and I won't be on speaking terms when we get to the penitentiary."

"What do you mean 'We'?" demanded the outraged Democrat.

"I believe," Quay replied softly, "that there are some strict laws against certain kinds of gambling devices in your city, as well as against certain other diversions. My information shows that you own most of these devices, with a number of ladies of leisure in the bargain, to liven things up a bit. The prosecutor is a personal friend of mine. Suppose I go down there and tell all I know?"

His opponent paled and departed in a huff but Quay had no more trouble from that source.

Penrose never warmed to the idea of holding a man's morals up as a bludgeon. Being himself somewhat of an expert in defying convention he couldn't scold others from straying from the righteous path. Not without being a hypocrite, and Boies Penrose was never that. Therefore he held up the bright side of the picture by promises of advancement, or on the general prospect of better times for the country. Better times for the country meant better times for all, especially for the parasites who lived off petty graft and protection. Penrose encouraged the breaking of conventional codes as a part of those good times.

When he wanted to carry out some design which required the help of a select few, especially if that select few were somewhat lukewarm to his scheme, he would stage a party in the Lochiel Hotel in Harrisburg. Such a party was always on an elaborate scale and left nothing to be desired. Absolutely nothing. It catered to the tastes of those on a level with Penrose and supplied an abundance of all comforts—rooms, food, liquor, music, women—everything. All expenses paid.

Such a party was staged just prior to voting on Quay for United States Senator. And of course the party had to reflect the importance of the job to be done. It was on a superlative scale—with Penrose at the helm, for he knew that it was not going to be an easy job to elect Mr. Quay. Every legislator was urged to be present, and with the exception of only a negligible few they all responded nobly. The revelry began early one evening and continued without interruption through the first and second nights and well into the second day. The members of that august law-making body were carefully shepherded to prevent their getting tired, hungry, bored, or leaving the hotel, and every member who could be brought, even by heavy pressure, to drink was liberally supplied with the very best. At the psychological moment they were all herded over to the Capitol where the members, being too befogged to think voted to make Matthew Quay Senator.

During all this time Penrose did not leave the scenes of revelry in the Lochiel Hotel, had no sleep, never refused a challenge to drink, nor an invitation to eat. He was the supreme good fellow and perfect host. Exaggerated stories are told about the unbelievable amount of food and liquor he consumed during those forty hours, the estimates ranging all the way from six to ten quarts of hard liquor, two stuffed turkeys, a half dozen chickens and a couple of hams, to —, but suffice it here to say that he kept his balance admirably and when the time came for a vote on Quay it was Penrose who seconded the nomination with such warmth and gusto and persuasiveness that the result was never in doubt.

Quay went on to Washington and Penrose, now virtual boss of Pennsylvania politics, at the age of twenty-six, began to celebrate in true Penrosian fashion. He was familiar with all the best saloons, eating places, and palaces of easy virtue in the cities of Harrisburg and Philadelphia and spent many days and nights renewing old acquaintances and forming new ones. He was so popular up and down the line that, according to reliable reports, his photograph, signed and framed, was hung up in a number of places alongside those of John L. Sullivan and sundry heroes of the sports world. When he felt the need of relaxation he had a large choice of doors open to him and many feminine smiles calculated to soften the cares of his arduous labors.

*Part Three*

YEARS OF GROWTH

WITH Matthew Quay in Washington after 1887, Penrose had ten years ahead of him in Pennsylvania in the official role of State Senator. Unofficially he was Quay's partner in charge of the province of Pennsylvania, and in those years, although he was subordinate to the influence of Quay, he was becoming the superior of the two in interpreting the broader phases of the political drama. Those years were of inestimable value to him for he grew to giant proportions in political strength and in the technic of manipulation which, in the years following, made him absolute master of the Republican party in the nation.

In an attempt to arrive at a just estimate of the Penrose traits and characteristics it has been necessary to interview many persons who knew him intimately during the greater part of his public life and who were in his confidence sufficiently to enable them to analyze the man's motives and the source of his strength. These estimates of him vary widely. Some claim that the man has been grossly misunderstood and maligned, while others are equally as emphatic that "the worst has never been told," and that it is impossible to exaggerate the baseness and perfidy that characterized the greater part of his public life. But a cross-section of all these estimates of Penrose, especially while he was confined to the State Legislature, give an insight into the Big Grizzly nature that is fairly accurate.

He was "the laziest man in the state," said one critic, yet he was an exceptionally well read man. He was constantly buying the newest books as they came from the presses, and upon visiting his living quarters one was likely to find them strewn all over the table, floor, and bed.

He was reserved almost to the point of snobbery, and many stories are extant picturing him as unwilling to shake hands with people. There was justification for such stories, as everyone who knew him admits, but his closest friends say that with those whom he knew and trusted his reserve disappeared and he was a "good fellow." It is true that he would not take the initiative, believing as he did that the great froth of friendliness exhibited by the mass of fawning politicians was at heart only froth and hypocrisy by which people sought favors and recognition. A political boss or leader is so frequently double-crossed that he must be extremely careful not to seem too intimate. It is also accounted for in part by the fact, in his own estimation, of his superiority which the advantage of heritage and class gave him. He didn't need to take the initiative in anything for the very good reason that others before him had taken all the initiative that was necessary for his success. Not only was he born a recipient of wealth, noble lineage, and high standing, but when he entered politics and became the object of Quay's attention he at once was the acknowledged Crown Prince of a political Dynasty that dominated the great state of his birth and had spread its influence to every section of the nation. He was a popular crown prince in spite of himself. He didn't care for popularity except as a political asset but the more he stood aloof and retired behind the scenes the more that was accepted by the rabble as proof of his greatness. But during all this time his unusually keen intellect was observing and refining the methods of control and manipulation used by others, and usually scoffing at their crudeness. Quay was superb at a certain type of organization, but when he attempted to gain distance with his own organization it proved rough going. Somehow it was cumbersome. Penrose took the organization that the Camerons and Quay had built up and made it superbly effective.

He was often characterized as "hard-boiled," but even a cursory glance at the rough aggregations he had to deal with, having to master hard-boiled outfits reared in saloons and back alleys where the code of the jungle ruled, demanding the use of tactics not altogether refined, it is realized he could have used no other. The times and conditions which produced Penrose demanded precisely the type of control which he gave in abundance. If it hadn't been a man by the name of Boies Penrose it would have been a man of similar traits with a different name, or else the whole political structure would have sunk into a hopeless deadlock of contending petty factions. No other type, given all the circumstances of the period, could have been successful in the jungle of politics in moulding the heterogeneous mob of rough-neck political pirates and determined business privateers seeking favor and place at the hands of an apathetic public. No other type could have wrought unity out of chaos and sensed the direction of power quite so instinctively as did Penrose. The time had not yet come for soft-spoken scholarship or ethical idealism to receive a hearing.

When he was elected President pro tem of the Pennsylvania Senate in 1889 he filled that position with an iron hand, and to the eminent satisfaction of his fellow legislators. He was frequently accused of being an autocrat in politics, but his friends point out, and with a good deal of justice that, despising double-dealing and hypocrisy as he did, he had to be heartless enough to cut through sham and persiflage to get at the heart of things.

Illustrative of the kind of unworthiness he had to punish, or, if occasion demanded, make use of, is the incident at Harrisburg related by a newspaper man of that place and period. "In the good old days," goes the story, "when bribery was often suspected, a certain orator in the House was converted almost in the twinkling of an eye from a violent opponent to an enthusiastic supporter of a bill. He was flailing the air with violent gestures, denouncing and lambasting the bill and its proponents, when suddenly from the rear a little man passed down the aisle and, without being observed, quietly dropped a small package on the desk of the outraged member. In a moment the overheated member went into reverse after a short skid, and without any apparent embarrassment continued in a different key, saying: 'These are the arguments, gentlemen, advanced *against* the meritorious bill under consideration. But so contrary are they to my own views that I beg the indulgence of this body a little longer that I may present the virtues and merits of a most commendable piece of legislation.' Having then argued as vociferously in the affirmative as he had a few minutes before in the negative, the alert legislator sat down, but soon thereafter he was seen to leave his place and seek the less public quarters in the rear where he might open and inspect the package dropped in the midst of his forensic efforts. It was a specie-ous plea."

The matter of his drinking and low carousals was always in the forefront of the discussions when Penrose's name was mentioned, but it has been pointed out repeatedly that a very great majority of the law makers of the times did the same things in varying degrees which Penrose did, but not as much was said about it. The latter was condemned, his friends claim because of his prominence. Penrose elected to ignore all such gossip concerning his personal habits for he held that since they were his own affairs and of no utter concern to others it was only little people, nincompoops, and reformers who noticed such things. He not only scorned to be secretive, and therefore hypocritical, about his passions and appetites but he refused always to use such shortcomings in others as a

AT THE HOME OF A FRIEND
On the Indian River, Florida

AT PALM BEACH, 1915
Samuel P. Rotan; Senator Penrose; Hugh B. Nesbitt,
newspaperman

weapon against them. To the end of his days he couldn't understand why society assumed the right to sit in judgment on anybody's private affairs. And of course he translated that same attitude into a stout denial of government's right to interfere in business and industry.

"Bah!" he would say in giving vent to his disgust, usually accompanied by an unintelligible snort. Then forthwith he would go to the stables, get his favorite horse and go for a long ride—alone. He had a Negro, as black as midnight, whom he called Freckles, to look after his horses for him. Frequently Freckles wouldn't get so much as a nod from Penrose, though invariably he greeted his boss with a broad grin and, " 'Evenin' Senatuh! Yuh sho looks fine today, suh!"

At other times the senator would stop and chat for several minutes with Freckles about the condition of the horse, its beauty and general demeanor, always receiving voluble assurances of the steed's intelligence and all-round superiority.

On one occasion after going through the customary ritual of greeting, Penrose was beginning to absorb the contagious eagerness of his spirited mount and chatted pleasantly with Freckles. He extracted a five-dollar note from his pocket and handed it to the grinning Negro.

"Here you are, Freckles," he said dryly. "Buy your wife a present with this."

"Thank y' suh, Mistah Penrose, thank y' suh!" said the bowing servant, smiling extravagantly. "But, Senatuh, you knows ah-ah-ah ain't got no wife."

"Never married, humh?"

"No suh! I ain't nevah marr'd."

"Ever thought much about it?"

"No suh, Senatuh! I's gwinna stay right heah an' takes ca'oh uv you and yo' hosses. Yas—suh!"

"Smart boy!" replied Penrose as he reached into his pocket

for another tip. "In that case here's another reminder just like the other one."

So saying he was off on his usual jaunt.

Although at times he was careless and indifferent about his personal habits and the consequences of them, he was meticulous to the point of severity about the minutest legal requirements and technicalities of any and all measures of a public nature. In resolutions, legislative bills, contracts, platforms, and the like, not a comma must be out of place, nor must there be a hint of a legal loophole. He knew enough of law to realize that its technicalities are often used to defeat justice or to give aid and comfort to an enemy. He drilled himself so thoroughly in all these things while in Harrisburg that even after he went on to Washington he frequently called up a gentleman still active in the government of Pennsylvania and his trusted adviser to inquire about the exact procedure to be followed in a given case.

This habit of accuracy and precision was his best wall of defense. Many times during his public career there were charges of graft, thefts, political rottenness, and investigations seething about his head, but none ever broke dangerously near him. Never was there a single charge proved against him; he had always taken precautions to fill all the possible loopholes.

The fact that he was so meticulous in his attention to political matters and that he could be trusted to hold the vote-getting gentry to his will soon attracted the attention of the clients of bosses.

And that was exactly the result he was working to achieve. He stood to gain not a single vote, nor to lose one, by making long trips to the hinterland of his state; people out in the back-water communities never voted for him directly. Not yet. What he was tremendously interested in, however, was in tightening his hold on the Organization by impressing upon every locality the absolute necessity of sending legislators to Harrisburg who would always be unquestionably amenable to the leaders of the Organization. By continually hammering away on this line, appealing to the legitimate self-interests of voter, heeler, committeeman, and legislator alike, a system as far removed from the blustering, threatening, individual wheedling of Quay, as anything could well be, he was able to build a shatter-proof machine that would stand behind him in every emergency. He succeeded in doing just that. Crooked wealth and crooked politics go hand in hand; one cannot exist without the other. Penrose played what he thought was a very necessary game of politics and played it in deadly earnest, but others with more ideals and ethics or more interested in them than in the game of politics called it crooked politics. Those persons and corporations with real money to spend were looking, as always, for some medium through which to function, and when they learned that young Penrose played precisely the type of game they liked they sought him out. At the same time he was being pushed into the center of the pool by Quay who, by this time, knew him thoroughly and trusted him implicitly.

The organized interests that got behind Penrose and bulwarked him handsomely till the day of his death were important in the order named: the liquor interests, steel, oil, and the railroads. After Quay's triumph over the famous "hog combine" in 1895, the leader of which was Governor Hastings, Penrose, Quay's major domo in Pennsylvania, could assure the dominant interests in the state that there could be no further doubts or interruptions to their program of control and that full steam ahead was the slogan. Just how gleefully those interests got behind Penrose with well-filled purses is reflected in the violent but futile protests of the smaller and more independent businesses of the state against the compact control set up for those few who paid the expenses of that control.

On February 2, 1898, four hundred of the leading business men from all over the state met in Philadelphia in a giant protest against the political domination which was always keeping them at its mercy. They were meeting to do something about it, but about the only thing that came of the meeting was a set of resolutions which declared, among other things, that "a large majority of the members of the Assembly of 1897 were nominated and elected by questionable methods, the chief end in view being the election of Boies Penrose as United States Senator, in accord with the dominant political influences of the state political machine; but the corrupt bargain carried with it the absolute control of legislation for all purposes. . . . It was not an unusual thing, during the session of last year, for the citizens of this Commonwealth to witness the humiliating spectacle of their own representatives wasting days and weeks, neglecting public business, because of the delays of their chief in giving them instruction as to what he wished them to do."

Penrose, when he read that, merely shrugged his shoulders and said that, "it is certainly too bad to see all that healthy talent going to waste."

In that same session of the Legislature something went wrong with the payroll. The monthly payroll of the House should have been $55,980, but somehow the figures got all confused and the appropriations covering the usual stipends called for $75,404, nearly 50% too much. Likewise the Senate schedule called for $39,480, but the appropriations covering same was $54,948. When a new and unsophisticated member "from the sticks," really got down to a study of the situation he "discovered the padding" and promptly introduced a resolution to correct the roll. His resolution was voted down by a count of 109 to 66.

The state printer, W. S. Ray, at the end of his first three months' work, filed an account amounting to $12,000. Governor Hastings asked his Attorney-General to look into the matter and report. He did. The report showed that the account was padded to the extent of $7000.

The previous Legislature had been toying with a bill to tax beer, known as the Bliss Bill. The public had demanded some such tax as the bill contemplated and the opposition to it seemingly was overwhelmed by public sentiment. The bill had no difficulty in passing the House, and it had come, at the end of the week, to second reading in the Senate. Just about everybody expected the Senate to pass the bill the following Monday by a large vote, but over Sunday something happened. Penrose's efficient lieutenant, the redoubtable Bull Andrews, rented a floor in a Philadelphia hotel and invited certain members of the Assembly to occupy those rooms over the week-end. Late Saturday night two special cars filled with leading brewers from all western Pennsylvania arrived in Philadelphia and the occupants of those cars hastened to become the guests, at their own expense, of the affable Bull Andrews at his hotel. The private cars that had brought the brewers kept their blinds drawn and a heavy guard around them, and any news of their arrival and purpose was strictly suppressed. When all those guests departed Monday morning the Bliss Beer Tax bill had been completely re-written and transformed into a Merchants' Tax bill which taxed everything else sold in the state except beer. In this revised form the bill was sent scurrying through both branches of the Legislature, and Penrose was solemnly but immensely pleased. Then Governor Hastings vetoed the measure, which caused Quay's jaws to snap angrily as he said: "We will own the next Governor of Pennsylvania." And it came to pass.

The results of this compact machine domination may be indicated, not only for state affairs, but city as well, by conditions in Philadelphia, where, in 1901, the credit of the city was so impaired that when it tried to borrow $9,000,000, all it could get was $5000.

These were the days of Penrose's most valuable schooling and he profited enormously by his apprenticeship. He mastered the technic of control, because "somebody had to be boss." There was not a single day, after he became President of the Pennsylvania Senate, that he wasn't virtual master of the state's politics. True, he had some opposition now and then, and the only political defeat of his career came after that date, but such opposition as came was directed mainly at Quay but hit Penrose instead. No serious differences ever marred the partnership of the two men, and anything which affected one touched the other. On his own account Penrose was master in his own state.

Thus early he formed the opinion which years later he expressed to his friend, Senator James E. Watson, that "Pennsylvania had to have a boss—just had to have one. William Penn was the greatest boss, both ecclesiastical and political, that ever lived in the state, and since that time Pennsylvania has never been without a real boss. A boss has to be hard-boiled and never yield to popular clamor or to private solicitation." That fairly well sums up the philosophy of Penrose and all others who make it a career to control politics and all the ramifications of a machine—politics is a private and personal possession and the public has no right to denounce its cruelties nor to judge its imperfections.

At the end of ten years in the State Legislature Penrose felt that it was time to obey Destiny's plain commands and become the mayor of Philadelphia. Accordingly in 1895 he set out to accomplish that happy result. During those ten years his popularity among the unregenerate masses had grown enormously; his opinion of reform and reformers had become more hostile; his orgies more frequent, open and defiant; his stature and cunning as a political boss was much greater, but his stature as a statesman had increased not a whit. He saw no need of growth in that direction. He had spent his days associating with cheap people—a giant among them—and his conceit fed itself enormously on their plaudits. He gloried in such feats as being able to consume four of five dozen of the largest oysters extant plus a quart of Bourbon at one sitting. With a load no heavier than that he could navigate beautifully under his own power. Or, perhaps his tastes would lean in the direction of a couple of stuffed ducks for lunch with the proper amount of liquid chaser and other ingredients. The crude fawners howled with delight at such accomplishments and Penrose felt amply repaid by their praise. Incidentally he added fifty pounds to his already enormous bulk. He was a Big Man to all his followers.

He knew his Philadelphia as few men knew it, from all the gutters to the City Hall, and he was confident of becoming Mayor Penrose. His cocksureness was inspiring. It didn't concern him at all that certain well-known citizens were uncovering an unusual amount of stench which was strong enough to attract attention beyond the borders of the state. For example, Middle Alley, one square in length, was the home of forty-four properties, forty of which were houses of prostitution to which, according to sworn affidavits of investigators, came three thousand visitors in one day. In the district between Sixth and Broad, Arch and Green streets, similar conditions prevailed. Then, there was that long stretch of city blocks reaching north almost from the doorsteps of City Hall and Independence Hall, between Eighth and Twelfth and from Arch to Spring Gardens, with additional bad spots on Pearl, Sergeant, and Broad streets, as well as in Soap-fat and Current Alleys, where the estimates of the time placed the number of ladies of joy for this one district alone at ten thousand. However, the peculiar phase of the matter was that in one election alone more than 80,000 good Republican votes had been recorded as coming from this particular district. And that was before the day of woman suffrage. But these things didn't disturb our aspirant for Mayor.

There was no particular opposition to Penrose, that is, among those who really counted—the bosses—and it was accepted as a foregone conclusion that he would be elected. But there was an angle of the situation which his shrewdness had failed to appraise. He was the protégé of Matthew Quay who, so people immediately concluded, would in fact become the dictator of Philadelphia politics, should Penrose be elected. There was a good deal of justification for this belief. Constitutionally the Legislature was made up of members elected from districts according to population. In an unpadded election rural Pennsylvania could always muster a larger representation in the Legislature than could be sent from Philadelphia. It frequently happened, however, by adding a few thousand votes at the proper time, the city of Philadelphia could hold the balance of power in the state body. Whoever controlled the city was master at Harrisburg. Quay was never in control in Philadelphia except insofar as his alliances with local bosses made him so. It was generally accepted as a fact that Quay and Penrose had such an alliance, and with the latter mayor, with that powerful machine going at full speed, the two would be invincible. The local bosses would still accept Penrose, but Quay —never!

Dave Martin, powerful local boss, garbage collector, fist fighter extraordinary and hater of Quay, quietly marshalled his forces and waited for the right moment to show his strength. Activities of the reformers soon offered just that right moment. The reform element was perennial but futile. This time it was following the lead of wealthy John Wanamaker, merchant prince and honest citizen, and drew in its wake the clergy of the city, the active participation of the leading women's organizations, as well as the better class newspapers. It was a set-up calculated to warm the heart of any astute boss to have access to a plentiful supply of Wanamaker cash and the active support of the reformers. Dave Martin had both. From whatever political angle one viewed him, he was as putrid a political racketeer as any of the long list which Pennsylvania has produced, but reform saw only the single purpose of defeating someone undesirable and failed to give much attention to the positive action of electing one who was desirable. They accepted without qualm Martin's handpicked candidate, Charles F. Warwick. The primary purpose of Martin and his wrecking crew was to administer a thumping defeat to Quay; that of the reformers was merely to defeat Penrose.

The plan of the campaign was to plaster the city with big yellow placards early of a Sunday morning which the church crowds and others read with wonder, amusement, and decent heed: "We citizens of Philadelphia ask for the nomination of a candidate for Mayor whose private life shows a high moral standard and whose matured character and experience in business affairs will insure a good administration."

"What the hell?" exclaimed Penrose when he saw that.

Quay became alarmed and went at once to Rudolph Blankenburg, wheelhorse of reform, about patching up some sort of "holy alliance" which would placate the good people of the city and insure their support.

"Would his joining a church satisfy these people?" Quay asked. "If so, he'll join any damned church you select."

As the campaign progressed Martin quietly swung his cohorts into line behind Wanamaker's crowd and waged a relentless fight. In the evening before the nominating convention was scheduled to meet, while Penrose and his army of retainers were laying plans for appropriate celebrations, both public and private, Martin and a few of his advisers called on Izzy Durham, Penrose's manager, and presented a virtual demand that Penrose withdraw from the contest. And to back up that demand they presented to the astonished Durham a "life-size" photograph of the excellent Mr. Penrose leaving a well-known house of prostitution at daybreak. A newspaper man came along with Martin to explain how the morning paper would carry that photograph on the front page with all the printable lurid details of this and many other escapades of the candidate for mayor printed just below the headline. This was too much for even a Penrose to ignore. Gossip and innuendoes might be laughed at and passed by with scant courtesy, but not so with front page pictures and articles in reputable newspapers. Especially if, some or all those stories happened to be true. Of course if Mr. Penrose could see his way clear to withdraw from the contest for mayor the newspapers would find something else to print.

Boies Penrose's name was not presented to the nominating convention the following day. Charles F. Warwick, a man inferior in every way to Penrose, except that his personal habits were a little less open to public criticism, was nominated and elected. The celebration of the Penrose crows turned to mourning but the supply of liquor consumed was about the same. The reform crowd celebrated and the city reverberated with jubilation, but it was not a reform victory at all. Warwick was acceptable to the machine and not a single practice of the notorious robber gang was altered by virtue of his election. Without boss Martin's help the better element would have been helpless before the Penrose onslaught, and with his election, Quay, with the former's help, would have crushed Martin. In either case the cause of better government in Philadelphia stood to gain exactly zero.

Penrose never quite recovered from that blow. He couldn't fathom the forces that could defeat such a superior man as he; couldn't comprehend the mental processes of any person or group of persons that would condemn to defeat a leader merely because of his personal habits. Always the hardest of losers, he couldn't digest his loss, and he never quite forgave Philadelphia for turning thumbs down on his dearest ambition. He "emerged from his Garden of Gethsemane not chastened, resigned, or pure in heart," writes an observer, "but more callous and insolent than ever." It was his first and only defeat.

The Penrose crowd was stunned, but they didn't remain inactive for long. Quay was furious, and when the Quay ire was aroused it was a force to be reckoned with. He set about finding a way to administer a stinging rebuke to Martin and the meddlesome reformers. Martin had assisted the "Hog Combine" to crush, or attempt to crush, Quay, but the latter was victorious in that fight, and he would continue to be successful.

In fact it was at about this time that the opposition to the continued domination by Quay and Penrose reached its height and its most formidable proportions. The "Hog Combine," as it came to be known, was a fusion of the anti-Quay forces in the state led by such local leaders as Martin, Mack, and Porter in Philadelphia, and Magee and Flinn in Pittsburg. In this same year that Penrose had suffered his defeat the Hog Combine

had made their most vicious attempt to ruin Quay. Both ep-
isodes were an outgrowth of the same fight. As bad as the
record of Quay was in regard to prostituting public office to
private gain, there was nothing, absolutely nothing, in the
record or attitude of the men opposing him which indicated
any improvement. Martin's gang was thoroughly bad. Magee
and Flinn had little improvement to offer. They merely wanted
to control the emoluments of office which Quay controlled.
The best way to insure that control was to seize the state
organization, and they proceeded toward that goal early in
1895. Fortunately there are still living a number of eye wit-
nesses to the most boisterous and dramatic state political convention ever held in Pennsylvania. Or, perhaps in any other
state.

As the big day for this convention finally approached, according to a survivor of that battle, Harrisburg began to fill all
its hotels and spare bedrooms with Republicans from all parts
of the state. What caused most disturbance in the minds of the
responsible leaders on both sides and consternation among the
peaceful inhabitants of the capital was the concentration of
hard-boiled fighters who had come to Harrisburg to defend
the claims of their favorites. Fist fights broke out like hives
on a baby. As the crowds increased it became almost impossible to distinguish who was fighting for what. On the night
before the convention was scheduled to get down to business
a great and ugly crowd of Magee's friends, supporters, and
thugs began to pour in from Pittsburg. They meant business.
At about the same time a similar gang of patriots of the Quay
camp surged up from Philadelphia. They likewise meant business. A great battle was in the making. Thoughtful leaders on
both sides began taking stock of the situation and, fearing
much shooting on the street the next day, with serious danger
to innocent bystanders, if any, and perhaps a riot, began work-

ing frantically for some compromise. As a peace move it was decided, at a midnight conference of the leaders, to rent the Opera House for the convention and that an equal number of tickets be allowed for each side. Only certified delegates should be allowed entrance. Word of the conference and its decision got around, somehow, and while a show was still in progress a number of plug-uglies of the anti-Quay faction forced the stage doors and began to filter into the wings back stage.

A neutral newspaper man was delegated to look after the seating arrangements in the opera house and proceeded there for that purpose.

"When I approached the stage entrance on Third Street," he said, "only after much shouting and pounding on the door was it opened a few inches, and I was asked profanely what I wanted. Finally the door was opened a little wider a long arm thrust out and I was yanked into the corridor, the door being promptly slammed shut. A large plank, cleated to the floor, was quickly swung into position to prevent any further invasion from the outside. I found the corridor more or less decorated with empty bottles, as was also the stairway leading to the stage. Men were lying about on chairs half asleep and mostly drunk."

The fight had been precipitated over Governor Hasting's attempt to wrest control of the state from Quay. The latter promptly announced himself candidate for Chairman of the State Republican Committee, and the fight of the century was on. After the "Battle of the Opera House," Quay was still in control with thirty votes to spare. With such an inspiring victory over the combined attack of his enemies from every section of the state, he was for the time at hand, absolutely invincible.

And now! His enemies would even defeat his great lieutenant, Penrose, would they? Very well! He would show them how weak they really were! He would make Penrose a United States Senator! All the Penrose followers were enthusiastic, but the announcement stirred no emotions in the heart of him who had been stung so bitterly by defeat.

After his crushing defeat in his pursuit of the mayoralty Penrose had no heart to tempt fate and risk a blow on the other cheek. Congenitally lazy and sluggish he preferred to remain among those whom he knew and where he could locate without effort the special brand of liquor and other delights which he demanded in large quantities. He had no desire to go to the United States Senate where he might have to make some effort "to get on to things." Besides, he had taken a rather loose-jointed organization from Quay ten years before and had worked wonders with it. The political machine, which for all practical purposes was Penrose's very own, worked like a powerful dynamo, and as noiselessly. The organization which Quay had handed over to him had worked more like a rickety treadmill.

When Penrose first went to Harrisburg, according to an old resident who was an eye witness to many sessions of Pennsylvania's deliberative body, conditions surrounding its daily functions were such as to make the meeting of the Legislature a horror and a nightmare to the people of the capital. The members were a pretty rough lot. An equally bad feature of the sessions of the Assembly was the swarm of corrupt and vicious lobbyists that always infested the city like a swarm of crow buzzards hungry for a feast. Legislation was accomplished by pressure which these lobbyists exerted on the legislators, said pressure being only a thinly concealed bribery by money or by other forms of unpleasant and revolting debauchery.

Penrose changed all this and refined the methods of his

control. The lobbyists disappeared and legislation was arranged through the boss, or his agent, and corruption took a different line of attack, though none the less vicious, efficient, or expensive. And after Penrose went to Washington his system still prevailed at Harrisburg. According to one observer herein is set down a typical picture of the Legislature in session.

One day in February, after the Assembly had been in session seven fruitless weeks, a messenger from Speaker Walton of the House was heard to ask, just before the hour of adjournment at noon, of a man known as "Clate" Erb:

"Shall we have a session this afternoon?"

"Naw; let 'em go home!"

And they went home, all of them, riding on passes supplied by the railroads.

Who is "Clate" Erb? you ask, that his word should adjourn Pennsylvania's deliberative and law making body? Simply Iz Durham's private secretary and man on the ground; the representative of the representative of the boss. Not an officer of the Legislature; simply one of Senator Penrose's sub-foremen!

Mr. Erb—no one at Pennsylvania's capital would think of putting any "Mister" to his name—was simply watching things while his immediate boss, Durham, was at Palm Beach resting during the four weeks that it was Mr. Durham's pleasure to enjoy the more agreeable climate of Florida—and the Pennsylvania Legislature did nothing but mark time and wait.

After organization in January, all the bosses left Harrisburg with orders to the 204 Republicans of the 229 representatives of the people to keep quiet and behave till Durham was pleased to return. "Clate" Erb remained, of course, to see that no legislation which concerned the machine should slip through. The legislative calendar was so shorn of responsibilities that important committees didn't meet except for an occasional card game to kill time. Decent members stayed at home, for they were powerless to do anything constructive, and many a session passed into history without enough members being present to constitute a quorum. One important bill was made a law although no legal quorum was present. As it happened this bill was of some public importance and interest and was being stoutly opposed by a small group of the better element. When some of the newspapers of the state commented on the vicious character of the measure, the Puhl Bill, a number of the members who were opposed to the measure investigated and learned that they were recorded as voting *for* the notorious bill. They rushed to Harrisburg to protest, but Speaker Walton roundly scolded them for being so slow to answer to their names at roll call, and ordered a new roll call. These same protesting members, answering roll, voted *for* the measure.

A good example of the type of "squeeze" legislation frequently brought forward was what is known as the Loan Shark Bill. This bill proposed to limit the rate of interest charged by these businesses to 6% annually. Now, anyone knows that a self-respecting Loan Shark would turn up his ample nose at a rate of interest of only 6% annually, even triple that amount, so all these gentlemen in the cities of the state met in solemn conclave to see what could be done about it. They soon found out. By making a sizable contribution discreetly to the proper leaders of the Organization the bill would be killed in committee. Regularly thereafter for a number of years that same bill was introduced for the sole purpose of extracting a few thousand dollars out of the pockets of the worthy small loan brokers. Finally the brokers became very tired of paying tribute to these legislative racketeers and refused to "arrange" for the bill's defeat. But this time when the vote was taken only 99 votes were cast in the bill's favor thus causing the measure's defeat. That would never do! That defeat had not been paid for! Instantly a dozen or more Philadelphians were on their feet protesting and demanding verification of the roll. Whereupon the Clerk, when called to a show-down, solemnly began to "verify" the vote and read 19 additional names as voting "aye," thus passing the bill. The Senate was even more emphatically in favor of the bill as reflected in the vote of that body. The pawnbrokers, by this time, realized their error and hastily got busy, and apparently successfully so, for when the bill got to the Governor he promptly vetoed it. Perhaps in the interim he had been "seen."

Penrose was well equipped with such little tricks as that. While he was at Harrisburg many bills on many subjects were ostensibly sponsored by him, for public consumption, then privately he would send word along to have a harmless little amendment, if not the Governor's veto, render the good piece of legislation futile. Labor legislation measures by the carload received his active support—in public—but there is scarcely a state in the Union where labor received less decent consideration than in Pennsylvania.

When Penrose was being groomed for the United States Senate, or more properly, the Pennsylvania Legislature was being groomed to elect him, certain parties in the state, looking back with satisfaction to the defeat administered to him in Philadelphia, figured that it would be comparatively easy to rescue the grand old State from any further debauchery at the hands of young Penrose. This was still in the days when Senators were elected by the state legislature. A candidate, therefore, had no direct contact with the voters. His constituents, and the only ones who paid decent heed to his candidacy, were corporations, and those businesses cultivated their spokesmen, the United States Senators, much more assiduously, than ever a popular constituency did its spokesmen. Since the election of a Senator was solely a privilege of the Legislature, that was where the battle lines were drawn. In the Pennsylvania body there were 254 members, of whom more than 200 were Republicans. The real contest was among the Republicans themselves, and it was among these that the reformers exerted their strength.

Dave Martin, a thoroughly unscrupulous and vicious political racketeer, got behind the candidacy of John Wanamaker for the Senate seat. Wanamaker had many influential friends and a large supply of cash, and Martin, as a few months before over the mayoralty fight, helped himself to both. He went among the law makers in dingy hotel rooms in Harrisburg, or in the quiet of their homes, at meal time or midnight, and in between, and dickered and schemed and bribed legislators. John Wanamaker, formerly Postmaster General in Harrison's Cabinet, upright merchant and citizen, teacher of the world's largest Sunday School class, must have held his nose frequently and shut his eyes at the unholy carnage. The battle raged furiously. Quay and Penrose were very much in evidence, the former, a battle-scarred veteran of many such fights, was directing the Penrose campaign and carrying the fighting mercilessly into enemy territory. Such desperate competition for the vote of the brawny, if less brainy, legislator in the ranks swelled his ego and sent the price of his friendly nod skyrocketing. Wanamaker was told that he could win the election for $400,000 in cash. He winced and demurred. Penrose was told that he would have to spend "quite a lot" to win the election. His latent talents for raising money were aroused. He boarded the first train to New York and returned in less than forty-eight hours with a quarter of a million in cash which he calmly handed to Quay.

"When that's gone let me know," he said simply.

He made other trips to New York where nearly all the most powerful constituents of United States Senators resided and came back with more cash. Altogether, it is estimated, he spent in the neighborhood of $500,000—and won the election. At that he had fewer than a dozen votes to spare.

Penrose was not particularly elated at his election, but it was a good pretext for a celebration, and he celebrated, magnanimously and effectively. In ordinary cases the revelry would have lasted for several hours; in this case it lasted for days. His servile followers had to be given due consideration and they lived up to their opportunity in grand style. When hilarity had reached respectable proportions Don Cameron, whose place in the Senate Penrose was to occupy, turned to him and asked:

"Boies, why don't you get married?"

"Sure! A little discipline would do you good," agreed the affable Mr. Quay.

Penrose considered a moment then answered in all the gravity a Senator is supposed to affect: "All right. If the Organization will pick the woman, I'll marry her."

The campaign had been expensive but not unusually so, only a half-million dollars or thereabouts, but to the senatorial constituents it was well worth the outlay to have the Penrose vote and influence on their side of the ledger. He summed it up for them by saying:

"Humph! You can't hope to take anything out unless you first put something in."

On March 4, 1897, Boies Penrose entered the United States Senate.

*Part Four*

SENATORIAL COURTESY

## SENATORIAL COURTESY

THE junior Senator from Pennsylvania was thirty-six years old, moderately stout, and good to look upon. His giant erect frame, now well filled out, carried all the poise and self-assurance of his aristocratic forebears. His dark hair crowned a well-proportioned face, and his dark, coldly appraising eyes gave the impression of one never caught off guard. He was one to attract attention in any group.

The make-up of the Senate in those day merits a moment of more than casual study. Although ninety men composed what was then referred to as the most exclusive rich men's club in the world its dominating power was exercised by a small group of a half-dozen men. The politico-economic forces, liberated and sent forth in wave after wave of industrialism after the Civil War, lashed against every institution and every standard in America with such corrosive force that nothing remained as before. During the three decades which followed, chaos and confusion gave way gradually to a sort of disordered order in which the outlines of the picture, not a picture of new human institutions, but the same institutions in new colors, appeared. And as the full scope of the picture became discernible, recognition of its details brought disillusionment. As the nineteenth century closed its books that disillusionment was everywhere in the land. With increasing frequency one heard the words or phrases, "bossism," "wage slaves," "peons of industry," "capitalism," "the Almighty dollar," etc., with a disregard as great as the misunderstanding of their true meaning.

The average citizen had supposed that the core of sovereignty was embedded in the Constitution, but when he looked for it it wasn't there; the seat of government, he thought, was at Washington, but when he sought it out it eluded him; American institutions were free, he had been told, but when he looked carefully he observed the mesh of bondage. If, as Schlesinger contends, the decade of the eighties marked the "Nadir of National Disgrace," it might be said with as much truth that the following two decades brought the Cult of Capitalism into its purest pattern. The Cult of Capitalism in Industry was paralleled by the Cult of Bossism in politics.

At the seat of government sat only the spokesmen for the "Invisible Government." Allison of Iowa, Aldrich of Rhode Island, Spooner of Wisconsin, Platt of Connecticut, Hale of Maine, and Lodge of Massachusetts formed the steering committee of the oligarchy of power the source of which was to be found in the powerful industries that were rapidly absorbing the wealth of the land. The ideal of government, according to these gentlemen, was not that which represented the whole people of the State, except incidentally—the farmers, laborers, clerks, the middle classes—but the powerful corporations. Aldrich thought it quite proper to refer to the various members of that body as the Senator from Sugar, the Senator from Steel, the Senator from Wool, etc. If an upstart from "out West" not completely identified with some powerful industry or corporation came within the revered walls of that body he was ignored, or treated as an intruder in the sacred realms of the mighty. To this select company Penrose was welcomed with open arms and soon became a member of the all-powerful Finance Committee of the Senate of which Aldrich was Chairman. The machinery of government existed solely to be used by corporate interests for their development. Granting of monopoly rights to a favored few to have dominion over the natural resources of the country meant creating great pools of wealth. Of course the crude and ignorant masses were used in the extracting process and some of the crumbs were allowed to trickle downward from the top to appease their hunger and prevent agitation.

Penrose had few friends, close friends; he didn't care for them. There were never more than a dozen Senators at a session whom he even respected. Among these Aldrich was the one man in the group who had his admiration and un-questioned support, perhaps because the views of Aldrich most nearly coincided with his own in the philosophy of govern-ment. Aldrich "had nothing but contempt for the notion that, in conflicts between the rights of man and the desires of property, the latter should give way," thinks Bowers. "He believed that a divine right to rule had passed from kings to property, and the motivating ambition of his career was to make his party the party of property. His policy was to mobi-lize, regiment, drill, and direct the property interests, and while he hoped to bring even the corner grocer into the ranks of conservatism, his eye was fixed rather upon the property interests—bankers, manufacturers, coal operators. These, in his dreams, were to hand down the law and the prophets to men of modest property-holdings. For the farmer he had scant respect, again following the Hamiltonian lead. To him there was nothing of greater necessity than maintaining the 'balance in favor of manufacturers instead of agriculture' which came with the overthrow of Jeffersonian democracy, and when the charge was made, in the debate on the McKinley Bill, that it discriminated in favor of the manufacturers against the farmers, he frankly admitted it.

"To the great body of the people he was utterly indifferent. He had a lofty contempt for the masses, upon whom he looked as inferior folk, easily led, easily deceived, easily betrayed. He was so completely scornful of these people that he found it repugnant to have any dealings with them, to notice their existence. So profound was his contempt for their vacillation that, when they misunderstood or misinterpreted his motives, he never took the trouble to disabuse them."

That attitude suited Penrose every inch of the way.

The philosophy of government, or more correctly the practices of government, for there was little philosophy in it, which permeated the nation in the last quarter of the nineteenth century and gave us capitalism at its best—and its worst— rested on the acceptance by the masses of

> The Delusion of Popular Government,
> The Delusion of Free Institutions,
> The Delusion of Individualism,
> The Delusion of Private Initiative,

and the general acceptance of Laissez Faire practices.

Penrose never entertained any doubts about the nature of our institutions and the ease with which they were made subservient; they had long been subservient to him in Pennsylvania. Popular government had always been a farce, in the minds of the American bourgeois class, but it paid splendidly in larger coupons and dividends than any government they knew anything about. Penrose never attempted to conceal his superior contempt for the masses and their gullibility.

At his birth there were only three millionaires in the United States. When he entered the Senate there were 3800, and the rate of their increase had accelerated to an astounding degree. According to one economist, Charles Spahr, one-tenth of the people owned nine-tenths of the wealth. The richest class in the country was composed of those who owned the mines, the factories, and the railroads, not those who owned farms and small businesses; and the swiftness of their accumulation was an achievement never before rivalled in history. It was the accepted vogue to speak of the Copper King, or the Silver King, or the Cattle King, or the Coal Baron, or the Railroad

Magnate, etc. This class was enabled to own mines and railroads and monopolistic corporations only by the fiat of government. All these things Penrose accepted as a fact. He never questioned the ethics of these practices and forces but set to work to control them.

The great mass of the plebeians, the nine-tenths who had been led to believe that they were living under the free institutions of a popular government served these Kings. For years they had accepted seriously the popular fiction that they were living under a reign of law and order and Constitutionalism. They didn't inquire into the methods by which the ballot box, symbol of popular government, had year after year been handing over to the unscrupulous, the cheats, and the franchise thugs, millions of the people's wealth without adequate return. As soon as a franchise had been secured, by fair means or foul, the doctoring began so that the returns would be much greater than was at first bargained for, returns which sucked from the lowest levels their substance. For example, the capital of the Erie Railroad in five years jumped from $17,000,000 to $78,000,000 by legal methods, but not a dollar of physical value had been added. The Louisville and Nashville likewise added twenty millions of "fictional" value in 1880. The New Haven in seven years increased its capital stock per mile of road from $39,083 to $103,424. Bonds and indebtedness per mile increased from $7,177 to $116,326. Its gross earnings increased over this period only 30% while its capitalization increased 333%. The same story could be told of almost every city or corporation in the land: the big and little magnates used the big and little politicians to accomplish these ends. It was rugged individualism hard at work. And while valuable rights were passing into these sturdy hands, the purchased politicians were at the controls of the machines which were grinding out in a steady stream, laws to bulwark and buttress every vested right against the day when the cry of the radical might be raised in the land. Penrose took second place to none in detesting the radical. But he also detested this vulgar display of all these cheap wealth-getters. He had a firm conviction, however, that there was no other method by which prosperity for the worker could be maintained.

The sweep of one generation, from Grant to McKinley, embraced a period during which the flux of ambition, inventions, subventions, idealism, raw selfishness, politics new and old, wealth, poverty, power, pauperism, produces a total impression all but impossible to describe. Although we are interested here primarily in the political aspects of the years in question it will not be out of order to touch upon contemporary manifestations of privilege as revealed in the tremendous surge to luxury and dazzling display, a display that drew from Penrose a snort of contempt. In the early nineties million dollar receptions were known, and a hundred thousand dollars was not an uncommon amount to be spent on a debutante party. A glittering banquet was tendered a small black and tan dog wearing a collar studded with $15,000 in diamonds. At one function cigarettes were not in presentable form unless they were wrapped in hundred dollar bills; at another affair fine pearls were given to the guests in their oyster cocktails.

In this lavish expenditure, thinks Beard, as well as in exotic performances, pleasures and excitements were eagerly sought by the fretful rich suddenly delivered from the bondage of labor and responsibility. Diamonds were set in teeth; a private carriage and a personal valet were provided for a pet monkey; dogs were tied with ribbons to the back seats of victorias and driven through the parks for display—and air. $600,000 was spent for a necklace for one debutante; $65,000 for a dressing table; $75,000 for a pair of opera glasses. Chorus girls bathed in golden bathtubs filled with wine to delight the guests. An entire theatrical company was taken from New York to Chicago merely to entertain the friends of one of the picklers of pigs, and a symphony orchestra was hired to serenade a new-born child. A Copper King from the West turned art connoisseur over night and bought a complete museum of art. In order to win the race of lavish expenditures the Bradley Martins in 1897 gave a ball in New York that dazed the Western world. "The interior of the Waldorf Astoria Hotel," according to a member of the family, "was transformed into a replica of Versailles and rare tapestries, beautiful flowers, and countless lights made an effective background for the wonderful gowns and their wearers. I do not think that there has ever been a greater display of jewels before or since; it many cases the diamond buttons worn by the men represented thousands of dollars and the value of historic gems worn by the ladies baffles description. My sister-in-law personated Mary Stuart and her gold embroidered gown was trimmed with pearls and precious stones. Bradley, as Louis XV, wore a court suit of brocade. The suit of inlaid gold armour worn by Mr. Belmont was valued at ten thousand dollars."

Penrose sniffed at all this. "Just a lot of silly peacocks strutting, but it's one of those necessary evils we have to endure."

One may decide for oneself whether these sprees of the magnates and the barons of industry, of the fretful plutocrats, of the stock and bond brigade, were any better or worse than those indulged in by Penrose, or whether they were merely different.

It was about this time that Senators Penrose and Quay, Izzy Durham, the Vare Brothers—George, Edwin, William—and a half-dozen other leading Philadelphia and Pennsylvania political leaders, organized the St. Lucie Club on the Indian river near Fort Pierce, Florida. It was known as a "Last Man's Club." Its membership was confined to a dozen men, with a provision that when a member died, title to his share of the property vested in the survivor or survivors. Senator Quay was the first to die, 1904. Ed Vare finally was the sole survivor. He died recently and the club is deserted.

It was extremely useful as a political club. There was plenty of boating and fishing and small game hunting, and drinking to be sure, but its greatest value was as a remote rendezvous for these political leaders, far removed from the stews of the political whirlpool. As soon as one campaign closed these leaders began planning the next one. Many campaigns were mapped out in this isolated club.

"Here you can think," declared Penrose, "without dressing up for the occasion and without being bothered by some whining lout who wants a job or a favor, and you don't have to bribe the damn fool to stop the whining."

Of all the qualities attributed to Penrose none is more beneficial to a politician than ability to judge people. In this respect he was far superior to the average in ability, but his judgment was instinctive rather than studied and therefore, to some extent, superficial. His opinion of the average person was very low.

"These nincompoops are not idealists," he said of a certain reform movement. "They call themselves reformers, whatever that means, but what they want is not reform but a few more dollars in their pockets. Put them in the place held by these other fellows they are trying to eliminate and in six months things would be worse."

He judged correctly that there were too many miniature autocrats in society to fight successfully against any sort of autocracy; too many potential millionaires—in hopes—to curb those now in power; far too many citizens with a boss mentality, from the housewife who bosses one maid, or a small store owner who bosses one clerk, to the factory boss who controls a hundred thousand workers, to eliminate bossism in politics. In short, every Tom, Dick, and Harry, under the stimulus of America's glorious promise of freedom and equal opportunity for all, expected some day to command millions of dollars or wield the big stick in the seats of the mighty. And they began at a tender age "playing" housekeeping, or store keeping, or commanding armies.

Most of the popular ballyhoo, he thought, was insincere and kept up by incompetents. But who supported them? Why, the rich merchants (Wanamaker was one of the reform leaders of Pennsylvania) and fellows like that who themselves want to be legislators, or own legislatures and make laws.

That the same logic, applied with equal force to the Gilded Ages and Tragic Eras, may not be so far wrong, was held by many. The excessive expenditures of the idle rich, the few thousand at the top, were condemned by the millions at the bottom not because the latter had higher ideals nor less selfishness, but less money to spend. If any given thousand persons, selected at random, were placed in the same circumstances as the few so roundly criticized, they would behave in identical fashion. Political corruption was deplored by the masses, but they didn't do anything about it because they couldn't see any direct benefits for themselves. Corruptions was a part of "the system." So were millionaires. In this free government "anyone is likely to get a break most any time, so why criticize the system?"

The dear people, according to Penrose, were filled with sweet hokum, which was much more palatable than hard facts. When their own leaders got a respectable following, enough to disturb the Organization, as frequently they did, it was merely for the purpose of seizing the offices for their own benefit rather than for making any deep seated changes in the laws. They merely wanted to place a different chauffeur at the controls. Not many of them would for a moment consider getting a new type of machine. And that was exactly the state of mind which pleased the bosses best. If the reform element became too strong, in Pennsylvania for example, it was quite a common practice for a trusted wheelhorse of the Penrose-Quay Organization to resign his position under them and announce, suddenly and dramatically, with plenty of news reporters present, that he had decided to renounce the whole thieving bunch of machine politicians and come out for the noble reform movement. Of course Quay and Penrose would fume around and shed a lot of "stage" tears. The better element would take such a deserter to their collective bosom and feel that salvation was just around the corner. When the stormy winds finally subsided and all the votes were registered, as usual, the erstwhile deserter and reformer would be found back safe in the arms of the Organization with a better job than ever—he had learned the inside secrets of the reformers and thus helped to defeat them. All stage play, but it worked.

Being a thoroughly good politician Penrose always avoided an open fight if it could be side-stepped. He was first, last, and all the time a lackey for Big Business. He gave unquestioning obedience to Henry Clay Frick and Andrew Carnegie. Mr. Frick was a stand-up opponent of all labor unions. He hated them like poison. If they so much as hinted at a demonstration Frick was for calling out the army to settle the differences—in Frick's favor, of course.

"Why shoot 'em?" Penrose would ask. "Compromise with the devils. Give 'em a little extra gravy till they settle down, then raise prices or the tariff to pay for it."

"Hell, man!" blurted Frick, "they want a hand in running my business. Give them a chance and they'll take it all. No compromise! Not with ruffians!"

"Mr. Frick, some day maybe you business men will learn a little sense. Meet them by indirection! All that the labor crowd knows is direct action and they are pleased when you capitalists use the same methods. Make a frontal attack and you're just playing right into their hands. All they want is a little more cash, not a hand in your business. Use your brains!"

Penrose was a master of indirection, chicanery, adroitness—in short in what he called smart politics. It required smart people to play smart politics, hence his contempt for the inept novice in reform who attempted to be a leader. The smart politician was always many jumps ahead of the reform leader and the gap between them seemed always to get wider. Only a few men ever graced the United States Senate who could play as smart a brand of politics as Penrose. It should be noted, however, that frequently what he and his kind termed smart politics was known by others as corruption, dishonesty, trickery, or deceit. To a politician all's well that ends well, while a more public-minded citizen might inquire into the methods used.

One example of smart politics as played by Penrose was the action of the Philadelphia Common Council, which he controlled. In June, 1898, it defeated by a vote of 52 to 50 a proposal to build a modern filtration plant for that city. Philadelphia for a number of years had had an annual death-rate from typhoid fever in excess of that of any other city in the nation. A new and violent outbreak of that fever in the northeast part of the city caused by the pollution of the water supply by sewage turned into the Schuylkill River, from which Philadelphia secured its water supply, caused a renewed demand for elimination of polluted water. The Council, by the above vote, postponed action for six months, thereby, in the words of the Press, "sentencing some 200 persons to die of typhoid, and some 4000 persons to suffer from a disease whose prostrating effects extend over a period of years." The motives for this shameful policy, which had been followed for years, are well known, said the Philadelphia Ledger: "The ordinance is antagonized by a combination consisting of factional enemies of the administration, supporters of private water schemes akin to the malodorous Schuylkill Valley jobbery. . . . A system of purification would have been introduced long before this if corruptionists could have seen their way clear to swindle the taxpayers in connection with it." Smart politics demanded in this case delay in order to wear down resistance and divide opposition and demoralize public confidence in order that the political leaders might better control the improvements.

Confronting the country when Penrose entered the Senate were momentous questions of national policy, questions that called for the utmost diligence in study and the earnest application of patriotic endeavor, yet about the first public utterance accredited to the new Senator from Pennsylvania occurred a year and a half after he entered that body in the form of an interview published the first of October, 1898, in which he castigated the enemies of Matthew Quay. The latter had been placed under arrest on a charge of conspiracy to rob the Peoples Bank of Philadelphia. Penrose took up the cudgels for Quay and thundered: "Attempted assassination of character has been almost the sole weapon of attack employed by Senator Quay's enemies for several years." The only thing Quay could talk about when pressed from all sides to explain the charges in his arrest, was to speak more feelingly than ever about the beauties of imperialism and brotherly love, or the little brown brother in the Philippines.

Quay's arrest for wrecking the Peoples Bank came as a surprise to many people of Pennsylvania, as well as to Quay himself. Not that there was any doubt in the minds of many honest Pennsylvanians as to his guilt; they were convinced in their own minds that it was true, yet they had no legal proof of it. The surprise was that he was actually caught. With the exception of about four years he had controlled the office of State Treasurer, if not the Treasurer himself, ever since the sixties when Kemble left that office. During that quarter of a century no effective legal resistance had been interposed to his misappropriation of state funds.

There were about two hundred banks in the State which received deposits of state funds, of which only six were on the "active list." They were the set-up banks and received the lion's share of the deposits. As a method of political camouflage the system of giving a large number of banks small deposits and depositing large sums in a very few banks, carefully selected, was excellent. For example, the Union Trust Company of Pittsburg had resources of $52,000,000 but received only $45,000 of State funds. That bank was too large to manipulate and its personnel was too large or too "independent" to be trusted with the inner secrets, but it was a well-calculated method of preventing criticism by keeping them sweet. A much smaller bank, the First National of Sheridansville, just a short distance away, was favored with a deposit of $100,000 which was double its entire resources. The Enterprise National Bank had a capitalization of $200,000 but received more than a million in state funds.

The Peoples Bank of Philadelphia was the favorite of them all. It was a bank organized by politicians and for politicians. "It stood for politics and rotten politics," according to Wanamaker, speaking at the time of the exposures. "It stood a corrupt combination between corporations, politicians, and public officers. . . . It has always had influence. It has profited by it. Organized by an ex-State Treasurer, it has always had State funds. It has continually carried a deposit ranging from $300,000 to $1,200,000 (its capitalization was only $150,000), while school districts waited in vain for school money long past due. It has held city funds. It has held other funds. It was a clearing house for personal profits. . . . Politicians brought their personal efforts to this scheme for profit. Public officers brought the public money intrusted to them. The bank received it, dealt in it, profited by it, and divided the spoils."

Unfortunately for Quay, cashier John S. Hopkins, when he committed suicide early in 1898, left a good deal of incriminating evidence in his unlocked desk. Among other papers was found this letter:

Commonwealth of Pennsylvania
Treasury Department
Harrisburg, Pennsylvania,
July 31, 1896.

James McManes, Esq.,
President People's Bank,
Philadelphia, Penn.

Dear Sir:

On Monday we will mail you check for $100,000, for the credit of the Commonwealth of Pennsylvania, General Fund, which will make a credit to our account of $600,000. The understanding is that I am not to draw against any part of this $600,000 deposit until the Honorable R. R. Quay has paid, or arranged satisfactory to you, the loan of $100,000, which you are to make to him next week.

Very truly yours,
B. J. Haywood,
State Treasurer.

The Hon. R. R. Quay was Matthew's son and of course beneficiary of the juggling method which involved at all times funds amounting to from eight millions to forty millions of state and city money.

Also this telegram was found:

"John S. Hopkins:—If you buy and carry a thousand MET for me I will shake the plum tree—

M. S. Quay."

The plum tree was the State Treasury and shaking it meant making a deposit of state money. Quay was an expert at shaking the plum tree and there always seemed to be a never ending supply of good juicy plums. Other cashiers before Hopkins had committed suicide after vicious entanglements with the Quay state funds operations but they never disturbed the judicious calm of the maestro. Hopkins inconveniently left some incriminating letters and telegrams behind. But of course the subservient legal machinery would iron all those things out!

Penrose threw his full weight into the defense of Quay and carried his politics of indirection into the court fight. All that was necessary for the time being was to secure from a friendly judge postponement of the trial till after the term of an unfriendly and moderately honest District Attorney had expired. The trial was postponed till January 7. The election by the Legislature of a United State Senator was due about the middle of the same January, and everybody agreed that it would look bad, in case Quay should be convicted, to re-elect him while under such a cloud. To show what could be done with a well-trained Legislature by two bosses who knew their business and their politics astonishingly well, they decided it would be best not to wait till after the trial of Mr. Quay to give orders to the great Republican party of Pennsylvania. They called a party caucus for January 3rd, just four days prior to the trial and instructed the people's representatives to vote for the Honorable Matthew Quay to succeed himself as Senator. The Republican servants of the people obeyed in caucus that command with commendable swiftness, but something went askew in the legislative session that followed, and for the time being they couldn't make Quay's election a reality. The vote was a tie, 79 to 79. That was all right, too, for didn't Quay own the Governor, William A. Stone? So the obliging Governor gave Quay a recess appointment to be U. S. Senator. But when Mr. Quay reached the Senate door he was refused admittance. Marcus Alonza Hanna of Ohio, next door neighbor to the Penrose-Quay principality, had now succeeded to the Chairmanship of the Republican National Committee. He not only gave himself large credit for making William McKinley President but, what is more important, he was the guardian angel of large steel and coal and railway interests in Ohio which were frequently coming out second best to similar interests in Pennsylvania. Hanna was furious and decided that the best way to place his constituents out in front was to cripple the spokesmen for the rival interests in the neighboring Pennsylvania, hence his hostility to Quay and Penrose. Therefore, when a made-to-order situation presented itself, Hanna was delighted. Quay, refused election at the hands of his own Legislature, presented his credentials in the form of a certificate of appointment from a subservient Governor and was denied admittance. Hanna saw to that. The vote in the United States Senate was also a tie, 32 to 32. Hanna cast the deciding vote—against Quay. It was now the latter's turn to be furious. Back to the Keystone State went the enraged Quay and Penrose and proceeded to rip into a "revised" Legislature with such fury and a large supply of cash that when the storm finally passed Quay was duly elected to the Senate with several votes to spare. Penrose had attended to that with the utmost finesse.

Then, too, there was the little matter of Quay's indictment on charges of wrecking banks, using millions of State funds for speculation, and trifles like that, yet to be decided. In the face of mountains of evidence to the contrary a subservient court of justice gave Mr. Quay a nice white certificate of acquittal and sent him on his way rejoicing. In the hands of a master tactician like Penrose it was all delightfully simple. Of course the fact that an escaped convict from New York and two Philadelphia natives with prison records were on the jury might have had something to do with the acquittal.

If one is inclined to think that most of these rascalities were due to the dominant Republican party, decayed by virtue of long continuance in power, or inferior morals, or to defective patriotism, let him reflect that the Democrats have had a good deal to answer for. It was Democratic ex-Congressman Sibley of Pennsylvania who led the fight in that State to have the Democratic legislators support Quay in his fight for re-election and vindication. The Democratic Representatives and Senators in Washington were urged to write laudatory letters to all who had a vote, Republican and Democrat alike, to support Quay for re-election. Senator Danial of Virginia spoke feelingly of the "spirit of broad Americanism of Quay." Likewise Senator Jones of Arkansas said: "In great struggles Quay has stood for the best principles of government." Broad Americanism! Best principles of Government! The dominant voting strength of Pennsylvania, headed these unctious encomiums. According to the prevailing concepts of patriotism in various times and places, the first and only requisite of a good American is that he give three hearty cheers for the Great Republic then retire for the night wrapped in the grand old flag.

To revert to incidents of a few years previous we find no improvement. Cleveland had a Republican Congress to deal with throughout his second Administration but the Democrats were sufficient in numbers to have held their political opponents in check. Instead they seemingly tried to outstrip the Republicans in making the era one of sordid littleness. The leading independent paper of the times carried this statement on March 4, 1897: "The legacy of trouble which Mr. McKinley will receive in this Cuban business will be left him, not by Secretary Olney or President Cleveland, but by the passionate and reckless Senate. That body has become the dangerous explosive of our national life." Another leading paper said editorially: "He (Cleveland) has stood alone between a rich and busy community and a horde of desperate plunderers, and beat them off. Not only this but he has maintained the public credit in the teeth of a legislature most of whose members were willing to betray it to advance their own selfish interests. Where other statesmen have left behind them a monument of wise laws passed, he left a monument of foolish and base laws prevented."

The succeeding Senate came in with a slightly changed personnel and, most observers felt, for the worse. It was this new Senate that Penrose entered. He looked at the material about him and accepted it for what it was worth, making no attempt to reform it nor to bewail its short-comings. It was democracy at its worst but he knew how to use it to his advantage; it was impossible of reform at that time.

The "legacy of trouble" which McKinley was heir to had to do with the Cuban question and the pending annexation of the Hawaiian Islands. The Sanguilly affair illustrates the state of mind of the Senate. Julio Sanguilly had been arrested in Cuba by the Spanish authorities and imprisoned, charged with incitement to rebellion. He claimed United States citizenship and at once Secretary Olney began to negotiate for his release which he succeeded in accomplishing. In the meantime, however, the Foreign Relations Committee of the Senate, John Sherman of Ohio, Chairman, took a hand in the matter. Early in February, 1897, an eagle-screaming resolution was introduced in the Senate which passed currently for patriotism and statesmanship. It read:

Resolved, that the Government of the United States demand the immediate and unconditional release of Julio Sanguilly, a citizen of the United States, from imprisonment under the charges that are pending and are being prosecuted against him in the military and civil courts of Cuba upon alleged grounds of rebellion and kidnaping. . . . And the President of the United States is requested to communicate this resolution to the Government of Spain, and to demand of that Government such compensation as he shall deem just for the imprisonment and suffering of Julio Sanguilly.

This resolution was debated at length and vociferously. The leading bloody shirt wavers in the debate were members of the Foreign Relations Committee, especially active being Morgan of Alabama, Mills of Georgia, Allen of Nebraska, Lodge of Massachusetts, and Frye of Maine. The very interesting fact of the entire episode was that the Committee in charge of this resolution had the following information in its possession before the resolution was introduced, namely, that said Julio Sanguilly had already been released unconditionally from custody by Spanish authorities, that his alleged American citizenship had been obtained by fraud, and that he had been out of America for five years and on Cuban soil.

Thus, Senator Penrose, during his first two years in national affairs, served an apprenticeship unequalled in the rich, broad circles of influence that played constantly about him. He had already won his spurs in Philadelphia and Pennsylvania politics and had learned well how to dominate any situation that arose there; it was the best proving grounds in America for aspiring politicians. He had courted and won the allegiance and respect of the ruthless Quay. He had won the respect and trust of powerful utilities magnates in Pennsylvania, New York, and elsewhere—C. T. Yerkes, F. A. B. Widener, W. L. Elkins, W. C. Whitney, Thomas F. Ryan, and John Dolan—and, far more important, he had learned what they wanted and how to get it for them.

On the large question of national policy, either of domestic concern or of foreign relations Penrose was eloquently silent. If Senator Aldrich, the Senator of the Sugar Trust, thought any stated policy was all right, if the Big Tariff Mogul, Dingley, agreed, or if Mr. Frick thought it would help the steel business or the coal business, of course it was all right with Mr. Penrose. He would work for anything they wanted; they *were* the Republican party, and that party was always right. He had no interests whatever in any questions except tariff and business. Satisfied on that score he absolutely refused to be bothered about anything, especially the skullduggery of the oligarchy of privilege which held forth daily in the Senate. It was much more pleasant back in Philadelphia anyway where he knew all the leading saloon keepers by their first names, and where he could find ready at hand ample satisfactions for his every appetite. Or at his St. Lucie Club in Florida, where he spent much time. But before leaving the august Senate to worry along without him he always reassured Aldrich.

"When the Republican party has decided on its policy, please wire me and I'll hurry back and vote in support."

His attitude in this latter respect was not unusual; it was typical of Democrats and Republicans alike in both houses. The prevailing thought and business of the times was profits for the large corporations to continue in office, and privilege for the politicians.

The exceptions to this general rule were so few as to be powerless in protest. It was a game of parcelling out the raw materials of a great nation among a few monopolies and making the public pay the bills. If the public occasionally raised a timid voice in protest it was silenced by Mr. Vanderbilt's gruff, "the public be damned," or Quay's cynical, "well, what of it? What are you going to do about it?" The masters could afford to take that attitude because the public was without any effective voice in any of its public business. Democracy, as it has been conceived in America, was never at so low an ebb, with the possible exception of the decade immediately preceding the Civil War, as it was near the close of the 19th century. The voice of the Progressives had not yet been heard in Congress, nor had the muckrakers put on their diverting and entertaining act. The waves of industrial expansion had finally beat against and destroyed the last American frontier, and the era of reaction and belt-tightening and "interior decoration" had not yet come. Instead the representatives of the Princes of industry looked about them for more frontiers to conquer. They promptly discovered two enormously important fields to engage their attention and talents.

First, there was imperialism and its two handmaidens—dollar diplomacy and Christian missions—and immediately the Hawaiian Islands presented themselves for annexation to the United States. Sugar had a surprisingly strong pulling power. Little Cuba needed the uplifting influence of our Christian civilization, and there were many other excuses for our growing dominance in the Caribbean area and for extending our dominance in the Far East.

Second, there was the far more important frontier of American mentality. Its complete subjugation was a stake of tremendous importance, and the Princes of Privilege were not slow to plan and execute the attack. To understand the battle and the victory one must fix firmly in mind that Americans were divided into the following classes:

a. Industrial lords and their bankers who looked upon our vast mineral deposits and other natural resources as entirely within their feudal realm and subject only to their command. This group was and is the governing class in America.

Approximately 3% of the population.

b. The Upper Middle class includes the investing groups—small stock holders and bond holders, independent business men, landlords, lawyers, and newspapers.

7% of the population.

c. The Lower Middle class—farmers, teachers, preachers, physicians, clerks, and white collar workers in general.

35% of the population.

d. Skilled workers and petty bosses.

10% of the population.

e. Unskilled workers, Negroes, and "foreigners."

45% of the population.

The masters in the first class coveted the wealth and power inherent in the possession and exploitation of the vast resources of the country. In order to achieve that happy end it was necessary for class *a* to ally itself with and work through classes *b* and *d*.

Class *b* furnishes most of the members of school boards, church boards, fills Congress and state legislatures with lawyers from this group, and edits the newspaper. If *a* can control these strategic positions in a society it can always be master of that society. Since the incomes, the very sinews of life, for the upper middle class depends upon the prosperity and whims of the big industrial lords in the top class, those in *b* group will fawn and follow any policy, however bereft of ethics, which the first group adopts. Our politicians come from class *b* but are only puppets of the top class.

When, therefore, the ruling class in America got around to shoring up and perpetuating their power and authority they had but to dish up a neat set of concepts containing their credo and pass them down the line for all the clans to accept. And accept them we did, hook, line, and sinker. Such concepts as:

Unrestrained competitive capitalism is God's greatest gift to man and it is a peculiar trait of American genius to make it work so well.

Americanism was founded on the ideals of freedom and liberty and any attempt to unionize labor is subversive of freedom of contract and, therefore, un-American.

High tariffs protect American industry, American labor, and the farmer. Farmers are the salt of the earth and they need no legislative aid nor tariff protection to make them prosper.

The poor are poor because they are inferior, and slums, mansions, millionaires, and paupers are natural consequences of free opportunity in a democratic society.

That separation of ownership from physical possession of wealth makes for progress and prosperity.

In labor troubles it is legitimate for factory management to call out thugs and private armies, and even the National Guard, to shoot down strikers, but it is un-American and criminal for the strikers to use the same methods and means to win their side of the argument.

Pulpit, press, and the classroom were urged on every occasion to indoctrinate old and young alike in the sweetness of the efficiency of Big Business; that democracy and capitalism are synonomous, and that any criticism to the contrary is Socialism or actual sedition.

And so on, ad nauseam.

The last thing this ruling group wanted was a free mind. They hated freedom of the press unless they could control that freedom; they forbade freedom of speech and worship unless they could make both redound to the honor and glory of their pet concepts. And it is high tribute to their genius that nothing contrary to their ruling credo has been tolerated in America for more than half a century. They bent the American mental frontier to their advantage as easily as they sucked out the cream of the American geographical frontier—till physical and economic dust storms befogged both.

Mark Hanna aspired to be dictator of American politics but never quite realized his ambition. The struggles of Penrose and Quay against Hanna's ambitions furnished one of the most interesting and colorful political battles in the United States Senate. It was thought by a number of his friends that Hanna was grooming himself for the Presidency following the close of McKinley's second term. But as a political ringmaster he had one fatal weakness—a conspicuous lack of tact and caution. It was this defect which condemned him to the role of second-rate politician instead of a boss of the first water. It was his gruff and unblushing boorishness which caused McKinley to become very cool toward him as manager for the second campaign, and made it necessary for a tactful but firm refusal to allow Hanna to take the stump in certain places in McKinley's behalf. He was too blunt, lacking most of the qualities of in-direction which gave Penrose such power and finesse. Years earlier Hanna had snubbed and fought the formidable Foraker in Ohio politics instead of placating him, thus creating a feud between them which grew as the years passed. He bulldozed his way through the local governments in Cleveland—and produced Tom Johnson.

He was a poor judge of men and notoriously inaccurate as an interpreter of events. When in the Republican National Convention of 1888 he put forward the aged John Sherman for the nomination and received the passive support of Quay and his Pennsylvania hirelings he supposed that support could always be counted on. The latter, however, had other interests. Quay was now Chairman of the Republican National Committee, and active manager of Harrison's campaign. It is note-worthy that in that campaign for the first time on so large a scale, Quay applied the Tammany methods and the Pennsylvania technic to vote getting.

Thus, Colonel Dudley, in his instructions to his subordinates, told them to "divide the floaters into blocks of five and put a trusted man with necessary funds in charge of these five and make him responsible that none get away and that all vote our ticket. . . . There will be no doubt of your receiving the necessary funds through the National, State, and County committees."

A. T. Rice, writing of the election at the time, said that there was presented "to the astonished gaze of the uninitiated the strange sight of voters being marched to the polls in squads of two, three, and four, under the direction of a trained party worker. In order to secure the proper casting of their ballots, those 'Independent' voters were there required to hold up their right hands exposing the ballots in the position until cast. The 'consideration' was usually five dollars, sometimes, lower, but often as high as ten dollars."

In this campaign Quay spent an estimated $5,000,000 to defeat Cleveland, but accomplishing that purpose only by the narrowest of margins. Out of more than ten millions of votes cast Cleveland had a popular majority of nearly 100,000. Hanna, in the first McKinley campaign, "spent $16,500,000, and there was no high cost of living in those days," according to Charles Willis Thompson in the New York Times, thus reaching what has proved to be the high-water mark of campaign expenditures.

When, prior to the second McKinley nomination, Hanna cast his vote against seating Quay in the Senate, he committed another of his tactical blunders which cost him his leadership and the loss of his prestige. It was a foregone conclusion that McKinley would be nominated to succeed himself, but what about the Vice-Presidency? Neither Penrose nor Quay was the least interested in any candidate, but they determined not to be interested in Hanna's selection, whoever that might be. Hanna had several candidates, among them Elihu Root, Secretary Long of the Navy, and Senator Wolcott of Colorado. McKinley had no special candidate but decidedly he did not want Theodore Roosevelt. Nor did he want to accept a candidate promoted by Hanna. However, he was convinced that it was best to accept the New York Governor as a running mate and work for his nomination for his own safety. Should the convention become deadlocked a swing might get under way toward the very popular Spanish-American War hero for first place on the ticket. In the meantime Platt of New York and the Pennsylvania bosses, Quay and Penrose, were throwing their support to young Roosevelt in order to get him out of the state of New York. He was a thorn in the flesh of the Platt machine, but as Vice-President he would be harmless. It was the work largely of Penrose and Quay that Theodore Roosevelt was made Vice-President.

Early in February of the year 1900, before there was much discussion as to methods to be used but a lot of speculation in the inner political circles, Governor Roosevelt issued one of those typically impulsive Rooseveltian statements which meant the opposite of what it said: "It is proper for me to state that under no circumstances could I, or would I, accept the nomination for the Vice-Presidency." And he added a sting meant for his chief political foe: "And I am happy to state that Senator Platt cordially acquiesces in my views in this matter."

Platt fumed. He most certainly did not acquiesce in those views. In a stew he went to Philadelphia to confer with Penrose and Quay about what was to be done. A part of what went on in this conference is recorded by Davenport.

" 'What you mean to say, Senator,' Penrose said, interrupting a bootless conversation, 'is that you want to force Hanna to take Theodore for Vice-President, but that you know Hanna won't if he can help it and that Theodore will balk because you want to get rid of him and is afraid he'll be just another Vice-President, a political corpse. . . . I am now going down to the bar for a breath of air. I'll be back any time you call.'

"A remarkable thing happened in the bar of the Walton soon after Penrose entered, seeking that breath of air. He called a number of acquaintances to him announcing that he had a little news for Patrick—Patrick being a justly celebrated barkeep who had served the Senator long and honestly.

" 'Patrick,' he said, 'You'd better look out. The next Vice-President of the United States will be Theodore Roosevelt of New York. If you don't know him, lose no time in learning. . . . Let us tremble while we drink.'

"When he returned to the conference above, Senator Platt was still fearful that it would be impossible to force Governor Roosevelt to accept the monastic office of Vice-President, from which no man since Van Buren had emerged into the Presidency, and from which men were wont to retire to abandoned farms.

" 'I went to college with Theodore,' said Penrose. 'I know Theodore very well. If you can get enough people hollering for him to take the job—common people, mind you, not nice people—he'll insist on being Vice-President. Just tell Theodore that the people need him in Washington and then start people out West writing to him begging him to take it. I've known Theodore a long time.' "

It was precisely this procedure, according to those who know—this policy of indirection—that fetched Roosevelt out of his reluctance.

Thus the first step toward defeating Hanna had been taken. Quay took the second step. Back in the 1888 Republican convention when Hanna was trying to get John Sherman of Ohio nominated, the former was located one day in the center of the group of Southern delegates. Practically every Southern delegate was there and Hanna in the midst of them with his hands filled with money handing it out freely to all who would accept—in return for support of his candidate. Sherman did not get the nomination but Hanna got the loyal support of a large block of Southern delegates. And he held that support through other conventions. This, Quay wisely decided, was the most vulnerable point of attack in the 1900 convention. He also had great prestige himself in the South among both Democrats and Republicans. When the committee on rules and order of business reported, Quay tacked on an amendment, which carried, materially reducing the number of southern delegates at the next convention. There was great confusion and consternation among the Southern delegates, and they appealed to Quay.

"If you fellows of the Southern delegations will get all your votes lined up for a vote for Roosevelt for second place on the ticket, I'll withdraw that amendment."

That statement started a stampede to Roosevelt and marked the end of Hanna's power in national politics.

The difference in methods of Hanna, Quay, and Penrose were as of three men starting out on a journey to a distant goal. On the road thither they come to a high and precipitous mountain which blocks their progress. Hanna, the man of forthright methods, would proceed in a straight line to his destination, blasting a tunnel through solid granite—if his supply of dynamite held out—and "get there in spite of hell and high water." Quay would call his army of retainers together in battle array and force them to scale the heights, himself on their shoulders, and finally descend triumphantly on the opposite side, though half of his men perish on the journey. They didn't count in the scheme of things, and anyway, it was for a good cause. Penrose would find an easy detour around the mountain and be waiting for his companions at the goal. No exertions for him, nor scars from rugged rocks.

It is significant that the Penrose method outlived the other two, and in modified form was dominant till the 1929 peak of prosperity broke at such high altitudes and toppled to earth with a great smash.

Quay was getting along in years but his fighting qualities were still good, and he made one of the most notable fights of his career, a fight with so much dash and fire that it absorbed almost all of one session of Congress. This time it was for his faithful friend of earlier days and staunch political ally, Bull Andrews. Of course Quay was to benefit, too. In 1901 Andrews was defeated for re-election to the state Senate from Allegheny, which event, some said, marked the end of Bull Andrews' career. But they had reckoned without the aged Quay and the redoubtable Penrose. They cast political eyes about them for more fertile fields and greener pastures, which they soon discovered, and within a surprisingly short time Andrews was on his way to the territories of New Mexico and Arizona to place at the disposal of those politically untutored people the benefits of his superior talents. Statehood was what they needed, and of course they had to have a boss to get the proper kind of statehood.

Before leaving Pennsylvania he had a million dollars of state funds deposited, subject to his withdrawal, in the Enterprise National Bank of Pittsburg. Quay and Penrose were to keep that fund replenished when, as, and if needed—out of state funds, of course. The enterprising Bull Andrews worked diligently.

He first set about securing a right-of-way for a new railroad that he proposed to build, which he called the Santa Fe Central and which proposed to connect the AT & SF railroad with the Rock Island. As soon as work got under way for his railroad he began his fight to have the two territories of New Mexico and Arizona admitted to the Union as one state, then have himself made United States Senator from that state. Senator Quay made a masterly fight in Washington to consummate Andrews' desire for joint statehood, filibustering almost one entire session of Congress to accomplish that end. If statehood could be realized, and if Andrews could be its boss he could have his railroad bonds validated.

Everything was working out according to schedule. Quay had enough support, he thought, to have those territories admitted as one state. In the meantime more money was needed on the railroad project which was secured by drafts on various Pennsylvania banks. Those drafts totalling more than three millions, were all honored, the security being more deposits of state funds to the amount of money withdrawn. Aside from that, Andrews' plan of becoming state boss was beginning to mature.

B. S. Rodey, territorial delegate from New Mexico to Congress, had long been an advocate of joint statehood. Andrews, wise in the ways of oily politics, became Rodey's worshipful supporter. When Rodey came up for re-election in 1903 he had such confidence in Andrews that he appointed him his campaign manager to secure a full slate of delegates. That was not very difficult, for Rodey was popular, there was not much opposition, and the resourceful Bull Andrews was an expert at securing delegates.

The night before the convention was scheduled to meet, every Rodey delegate switched his allegiance and became an Andrews delegate, and they nominated him instead of Rodey —an old Pennsylvania custom. Bull was accordingly elected territorial delegate to Washington and at the same time had himself replace Mr. Frank Hubbell as Republican boss of New Mexico, a brand of Pennsylvania politics new to the western states.

But Quay's efforts came to naught and joint statehood had to be abandoned; so did Bull's ambition to be United States Senator.

Quay had fought his last political battle—and lost.

The Senate which Penrose entered in 1897 witnessed a number of significant changes emerge toward the center of the stage. The two decades from the Hayes-Tilden contest to the silver campaign of Bryan were years of "The Great Calm," in which no major change or political philosophy challenged the prevailing forces. Deep under the surface, however, strong currents were being felt. The tools of industry and instruments of production were passing out of the hands of individual workers into the grasp of individual capitalists. At the same time the relations between employer and employee changed, many people thought for the worse. Since capital, accumulated days labor, was more elastic and pliable than individual workers, capital became everywhere an instrument of advantage over the worker. To offset the advantage gained by this new phase of capital, labor banded together for its own protection and an issue was joined which bulks large in the present social revolution. Panic after panic followed this change in relations, and everywhere panics were followed by strikes, some of which stand out as blackened landmarks in this terrible struggle—Homestead, Leadville, Haymarket, Pittsburg, and a thousand lesser ones. There were no Simon Legrees so long as the relationship between slave and master was direct and personal. It was when the once kind master grew in opulence and sought luxury in the cities, leaving his plantation in the charge of overseers that Simon had his chance. So it was with industry.

Soon the individual capitalist staggered under his load and gave way to another form of absentee landlordism applied to capital. The Trust came, then the giant holding company took its place, and the once powerful individual capitalist became only a cog in the machinery. His capital was managed by the distant manipulator of credit, giving us the Simon Legrees of credit capitalism—the Morgans, Insulls, Mitchells, Rockefellers.

In the realm of politics similar changes took place. First the individual leader, then the boss, and last the corporate control of politics, or the system. The politics in Booneville were controlled by the boss sitting in New York or Philadelphia. The powerful capitalists, or a group of them, at first sent their representatives to the city council, to the State Legislatures, or to Congress. These representatives became bosses in their various realms, from the village boss to the national boss, with many assortments of bosses in between. Big Business had its pleader in every court and on every Congressional committee. This procedure became expensive and finally Big Business became the courts and committees.

Of Penrose's colleagues in the Senate when he first entered that body, more than half of them were independently rich, many of them millionaires many times over. If the wealth owned outright by the ninety Senators at that time had been spread equally among the members of that body each member would have had nearly three millions. If the corporate wealth and business represented directly by counsel as well as by direct ownership had been massed it would have represented 87% of the corporate business of the United States—all directed from Washington. The individual was lost in the mass.

It is natural, therefore, that the business of the Senate was devoted quite largely to the interests of Big Business. Nothing else mattered. McKinley, as Chairman of the House Ways and Means Committee, worked for the highest and in many respects the most destructive tariff in history, and according to John T. Flynn, "framing the McKinley Bill made one of the most disgraceful chapters in American history. McKinley called in representatives of the various special interests to be favored and told them to write out their own schedules. Advice was asked of no one else. Even so orthodox a protectionist as Blaine drew back from the surrender."

Penrose, a few years later, as a member of, and later Chairman, of the powerful Finance Committee of the Senate, carried out a more perfect system of tariff making which would produce "more protection and less noise." After the tariff was taken care of and other matters touching upon a few big industries of the country Penrose was content. Once when good-naturedly taken to task for not giving more heed to statecraft, he was surprised and indignant.

"What the hell? What else is there worth looking after? All the little fellows? Humph! That's the trouble now—too many little fellows always yelling for somebody to give 'em a dime! Listen, you! All the help in the world won't make a big man out of a little fellow."

At another time when a prominent newspaper man from Philadelphia, Dr. Talcott Williams, was hinting in the same vein that he should pay more heed to the welfare of the people and work along a higher plane of statesmanship, Penrose's reply was characteristic.

"What's the use? I propose to be Senator. I want power. It's the only thing I crave. I have it. I shall keep it. There are about 5000 election divisions in this state. They hold from 20,000 to 25,000 Republican workers who carry divisions and bring out the vote. I must know all these men. They must know me. If I do not meet them and never see them, I must know who they are, and what they want, and how and when. My hand must always be on the job. I can never take it off; if I do I'm gone. The interests of the State? Of course I look after those. But the job is knowing and managing the 25,000 men who run the election divisions. As for great measures and great issues such as you talk about no Senator of a state this size, run as it is, has the time to take them up. I am always glad to hear suggestions. Come to me, write to me. I shall always be glad to hear you, but staying Senator is my job."

In examining the soil and climate which produced Penrose the student at once is impressed by the passionate cynicism with which denunciations were hurled at those few timid souls who challenged the steady onward sweep of corporate control. Anyone who questioned the divine right of the new capitalistic managers to full control of government was bludgeoned into silence as a "wild radical," or a mere "theorist," or a despised "reformer." During the last quarter of the nineteenth century and the first few years of the new we were too much in the center of the whirl to get an accurate sense of direction. We couldn't realize then the steady shift into classes of the American people and the constantly downward trend of the standard of living. In 1933 we obtained a clearer conception of these major movements.

As the plutocracy shot upward into power and glamour above the low social plane of a generation before it centered in great cities and built palatial homes on Fifth Avenue or great mansions near the water front. Back of the avenues and the water front were slums and crowded quarters of the ever-increasing army of retainers and caterers; surrounding the factories huddled the ever-enlarging mass of foreigners and cheap labor competing with one another for bare subsistence, all the while pouring enormous profits into the hands of the mighty barons of capital. The office holder, small and large, became as much a caterer and server of the financial potentates as was the lowest menial. Immigration in a steady stream from the lowest classes of Europe was constantly encouraged by the plutocrats to provide always a plentiful supply of cheap labor. Cheap labor applied to cheap raw materials made great profits possible, and "cheap politics" provided both elements.

It was at this point that Penrose found his greatest field of usefulness. Being an aristocrat, born to wealth, class and position, he cared naught for the emoluments of office, but he cared tremendously whether aristocrats ruled the country or whether it should be turned over to the rabble. The aristocrats of birth and class had withdrawn from the field but the aristocrats of the dollar had swarmed in and taken his place, and to this class Penrose gave his unstinted support. They in turn gave him their confidence and praise. When they wanted things done, being too busy to grope through the impenetrable maze, they called in the services of this master of devious processes and he directed them unerringly to their goal.

If the man in "big money" wanted a franchise to build a street railway he called in the boss who knew how to "see" the Aldermen and arrange for the necessary monopoly rights. Of course the Aldermen could always exact and receive favors from the great magnates; Penrose saw to that, too. These favors percolated downward so that all who served might share. The whole swing of affairs turned in the direction which made it easy for the master of wealth to continue upward. His servers included the law making machinery, the law enforcing coterie, and the law interpreting contingent. So, all these retainers of the Great Khan followed him solicitously wherever he went, whether in absorbing monopoly rights in copper, water power, steel, aluminum, or sugar, and they made his reign prosperous and happy by rendering good service with becoming adulation. Whatever he did was both right and legal. The King could do no wrong!

Penrose affected to believe that public office was the last refuge of the incompetent, and that anyone seeking office was so inefficient that he was unable to make a living by his own efforts, hence his love for a tax supported payroll. That applied particularly to the reformers who merely wanted the office the other fellow had only for the sake of the office. It is an easy step from that belief to his deep scorn for any person who stooped to pick up the small pocket change of graft in politics. He had only contempt for many of Quay's tactics and frankly said so—much to the latter's chagrin.

When Penrose stoutly affirms that he never profited so much as one dollar from politics one is inclined to believe him. He was one of those fortunate individuals who never had to concern himself about acquiring money. His father owned most of the water front at Atlantic City, before any city was there and profited enormously by the rapidly increasing values. The Shelburne hotel and other valuable properties occupied land belonging to Boies' father. He also had heavy interests in the street railway development in Philadelphia. Boies shared handsomely in this income after the death of his father, Dr. Richard Penrose. He organized the Denver-Utah Copper Company from which he received an annual income of $84,000 a year. His hand was dominant in the Southern Transit Company. Although his income annually was well over a quarter of a million dollars, at his death his wealth was less than that of any of his brothers, being about $7,000,000. Being a bachelor he never had the expense of a family. His expenses were no greater than those of the average Senator, some of whom maintained as many as three homes. He spent little or nothing on gambling or travel or expensive hobbies. He maintained no elaborate establishments to be pointed out to sightseers. Nelson Aldrich sold his entire business holdings in the early years of his public life for about $50,000 and gave his full time to being United States Senator, but within a dozen years his fortune was reputed to have passed the ten million mark. Quay made millions out of politics. Many other men have done the same thing. Not so Penrose. Money as such meant nothing whatsoever to him. He didn't need to depend on his salary for a living and it was his theory that only that type had a right to hold office.

Legislation should proceed, according to his theory, on the basis of what was best for the big fellows. If they could be made prosperous naturally they would pass that prosperity on down to the little fellows. If Henry Clay Frick called, Penrose would at once get the fastest train to Pittsburg and give obedient heed to what the great one had to say. If John D. Rockefeller of Standard Oil wanted a favor, Penrose would see to it. Or if the Pennsylvania Railroad Company, or the coal operators, or the steel mills called, Penrose would speed to heel and give obliging service. By giving these large employers every attention and keeping the mills operating at maximum speed and capacity, freeing them from as much of the tax burden as possible, raising tariff for them, reducing government regulations, they would pass that prosperity on to a maximum number of workers in the form of wages. That was his conception of working for the people and he could envision no other. To a friend who had playfully chided him for his lack of interest for the common people, he snorted his contempt.

"By God, the common people are at work, aren't they? Who pays the wages? And who gives them a chance to earn them? The men who own the factories, of course. And who helps the owners of these factories get business and make profits so they can pay these wages and all the taxes the little fellow can't pay? I do. I work hard for the people and so does every other man in Congress who is worth a damn. There's a lot of demagogs that do nothing but talk about what they are going to do. Work for the people? Humph!"

He was utterly unable to see why there was any hint of wrongdoing when years later someone uncovered a letter to him written October 13, 1904, and signed by John D. Archbold, Treasurer of the Standard Oil Company, in which Mr. Archbold wrote:

"In fulfillment of our understanding, it gives me great pleasure to hand you herewith certificate of deposit to your favor for $25,000, and with best wishes. . . ."

Well what of it? Certainly he had accepted the $25,000 from the Standard People! He would accept money from any body who was willing to pay for services. That donation was for use in keeping the great Republican party in good condition, and that party was the one that ran the Government, wasn't it? The Government enabled them to do business at a good profit, didn't it? Why shouldn't those big fellows pay to keep the Government running? He didn't use the money for his own pleasure; it was used to keep the political machinery running. How else could the Government keep going?

When Samuel Gompers, President of the American Federation of Labor, went to enlist the help of Penrose in putting through Congress some child labor legislation, the latter was very attentive and sympathetic. He really believed children ought to be kept out of factories. But Penrose couldn't support child labor legislation, for such an act would damage the prosperity of the mills, those same mills whose owners gave $200,-000 a year to the Republican party for the single purpose of protecting the mills against possible governmental interference, low tariffs, and higher taxes.

The period of Penrose was a period when independence of thought and action was at an incredibly low mark in America.

The Penrose-Quay outfit in Pennsylvania, about 1895, controlled much of the news reporting machinery of the larger cities of the state. One journalist, active at that time, is authority for the statement that in Philadelphia an insider in the offices of the telegraph company conveyed information to Penrose on any and all telegrams received or sent out that had any possible political significance. Besides owning outright certain organization papers over the state, there was always a friendly reporter who was admitted to the inner circle of the organization. Any reports turned into his paper had to be harmless, even though the policy of the paper was antagonistic to the organization. When the report reached the re-write man it was again in the hands of a friend. By the time the report—any report about politics—reached the reader on the streets it was either complimentary to the organization or it was vapid. Likewise it was so managed that seldom did an Associated Press story get on the wires of which the machine gang hadn't first approved.

Once it was thought necessary to control press, pulpit, and educational institutions to prevent King George III being praised on this side of the Atlantic, and to cement public opinion and deed into a weapon of statehood which could successfully meet the challenge of European aggressors. After all such dangers had passed, after the Civil War had thrown all public control into the hands of a small industrialist group, the same methods were used to prevent criticism of that control. Capitalism flourished. To prevent too much criticism of the system which capitalism was forging, it became necessary to control press, pulpit, and educational institutions. And that control reached its full stride during the period under consideration.

One staunch friend and supporter of Penrose was Congressman Joseph C. Sibley of Pennsylvania. He was a strong supporter in that state of the prevailing high tariff, protected industries, controlled press, etc., despite his party affiliations, and rendered valiant aid to the cause of proper "education." As such he was of peculiar interest to the Standard Oil Company, as the following letter, written in 1905, indicates.

> Joseph C. Sibley, Chairman,
> House Committee on Manufactures
>
> Washington, D. C.,
> March 7, 1905

My dear Mr. Archbold:

The illness of Mrs. Sibley has prevented my coming to New York. Senator B. was to have gone over with me. I think he will go anyway, as he has business there. I had a conversation with an important "official" yesterday and he told me that there was but one thing to do and that was to start a "backfire." Like myself, he is much alarmed, and as an official of the reigning family his hand and tongue are tied.

He thinks the work should be done in the *education* of public sentiment between now and the meeting of Congress in October. It has, I think, been decided to convene Congress in Extra Session at that time, though the Speaker will try to have it go over until November if he can't do better. I will know in a day or two how he succeeds. Long (Senator) and Curtis (Representative) are the strong men in the Kansas delegation. I have *explained* matters to them and I think their influence will count some when they go home. Campbell is a clever boy, has no strong points on place yet developed, he seeks notoriety, but is harmless in himself. This agitation, in the language of another, "started from the top," and will run its course. It is not a deep-seated and profound conviction of wrong.

The one thing is to get delay until temperate action can be secured, we will recover from Lawsonitis if we get pure air for a while.

I think the pendulum will swing to the other side after a while but I don't want the devil to pay before it gets back. *An efficient literary bureau is needed, not for a day or a crisis but a permanent and healthy control of ASSOCIATED PRESS and kindred avenues.* It will cost money but it will be the cheapest in the end, and can be made self-supporting. The next four years is more than any previous epoch to determine the future of this country. No man values public opinion or fears it so much as Roosevelt. No man seeks popularity as much as he. *Mild reproof or criticism of his policies would nearly paralyze him.* Today he hears only the *chorus of the rabble*, and he thinks it is public sentiment. I don't know whether the Industrial Corporations and Transportation Companies have enough at stake to justify a union of forces for concerted action. It seems to me necessary. I am in a position where I see both sides of the game and still think our friends play politics once in four years while the other side play it all the time. (All italics mine.)

Sincerely yours,<br>Sibley.

The Standard Oil Company, as well as all other corporations of that time, and since, were thorough believers in "education" as one indispensible function of free government. Of course it was their aim to determine the type and nature of that education. Prof. George Gunton published Gunton's Magazine at 41 Union Square, New York, in which he sang one continuous Hallelujah Chorus to Big Business. Not only that, he had an ambitious scheme to form a syndicate reaching the entire reading public so all would be aware of their many blessings. Big Business paid well for such services, and paid annually.

My dear Professor:

Responding to your favor it gives me pleasure to enclose you herewith certificate of deposit to your favor for $5000., *as an additional contribution* agreed upon to aid you in your most excellent work. I most sincerely hope that the way will be open for the *larger scope* as you anticipate.

Very truly yours,<br>John D. Archbold.

The same corporation also paid $5000 for a three-dollar yearly subscription to Thomas F. Grasty's Southern Home Magazine which reached the farmers of the South. It did noble missionary work among all the voters it reached in building up a kindly attitude of acceptance of the Standard Oil Company in particular and of all corporations in general. Such methods of impressing the mental pattern of the masses while it was in a formative stage and of implanting a positive concept was of tremendous value in neutralizing the opposition which some office-seeker might try to create. The voter, with his opinions previously set, would pass off contrary protests of legislators as merely playing politics. To a notable degree the muckrakers were neutralized before they began their work.

A Massachusetts schoolmaster in 1885 had to sign, as a part of his contract, a statement designed to satisfy the most fastidious sentiment in any community in the matter of patriotism and Americanism. It follows in part:

"I do solemnly swear or affirm . . . that I will uphold the Constitution of the United States, will not engage in nor tolerate subversive criticisms of the institutions under its protection, will revere the patriots who have fought to uphold it. . . ." Under its protection, depending, of course on who did the interpreting, children were being denied their right of the pursuit of happiness, were being worked outrageously for a mere pittance, labor leaders were being jailed by courts of justice, strikers were being shot down, and the much heralded American standard of living was being sapped by the greed of the masters of the credit structure of the nation. Yet no tax-paid employee was allowed to criticize or tolerate criticism of the scheme. Penrose was aware of all this and regretted it, but it was one of those necessary evils in getting things done.

LEIGHTON C. TAYLOR
Secretary to the late Senator Penrose

Penrose was fully aware of the demagogery behind the pretensions and froth of those in control.

"What the hell do you mean by that 'point with pride,' General?" he demanded, according to Davenport, of General Bingham, who for years had represented the Union League of Philadelphia in Congress.

" 'Point with pride?' protested the stuffy little Congressman. 'Point with pride? What do you mean?'

" 'Last night at the State convention, in your speech,' explained Penrose, 'you were pointing with pride all during your speech.'

"The General wheezed a bit and then tried scoffing the question off. Surely Mr. Penrose understood. It was nothing, nothing. A mere figure of speech. Penrose looked disappointed.

" 'General,' he said, 'We're a hell of a lot, aren't we?'

" 'Why, Mr. Penrose, why?'

" 'Always pointing to nothing with pride?' "

Nevertheless Penrose firmly believed that wealth, its source and machinery of accumulation, by natural right, should fall into the hands of those who were strong enough to seize it and hold on to it. That class had superior brain power to administer it wisely. Likewise, he sincerely believed that "the people" were not capable of administering governmental affairs, meaning the privilege which wealth and position confer, and that in reality they didn't crave that right. All they wanted was more pay on Saturday night with sufficient opportunity of enjoying that extra pay. He used his influence in 1890 to defeat every attempt to liberalize the Sunday blue laws of the State on the theory that the rank and file of citizens shouldn't enjoy too much freedom and liberty. The masses had to be kept within pretty narrow bounds. For the masters it was different. They might enjoy all the liberty and freedom they could seize. However, not only did the common run of people tolerate the vagaries of the rich and powerful; they imitated them. The raucus, crass, and bibulous jamborees of the rich found a counterpart at every level down to the bottom.

"Education? Sure, I'm for education," answered Penrose, in response to a question, "up to a certain point. People should be taught to read so they can enjoy themselves. Naturally they ought not to be allowed to take up with every freak idea that some of these high-brows disseminate. A lot of them are dangerous to public safety."

He was an active exponent of the practice of spreading illusions about democracy while withholding its substance. The financial monarchization of government after the Civil War went on apace while preachments of the demagog praised the virtues of democracy. Reactionary and imperialistic practices everywhere sapped the substance of democracy and concentrated the control of wealth in the hands of an industrial feudalism. This was made particularly easy in America because of the fluidity of classes. The growth of corporate enterprises made it easy to distribute widely a few shares of stock and occasionally a bond and made easy of acceptance the idea that anyone could become a captain of industry by the simple process of working hard, attending to one's own business, and investing the surplus in the corporation. Thus the commonest wage earner could have a voice in the control of industry.

Penrose was quite largely responsible for another method of control. In almost every small city of the country, to say nothing of the larger centers of population, one or more of the rising young attorneys would be retained by some corporation to do an errand, render an opinion, or look after its local interests, thus indirectly bringing the entire profession of law into sympathetic relationship with Big Business. De Tocqueville thought that this type of modern commercial feudalism of wealth is more dangerous and more potential of evil than chattel slavery, because it permeates all sections of the nation and has its ramifications in every opinion-forming center of society.

Penrose saw all this; had created much of it; was the master of it, but did not fear the revelations of muckraking. He was so versatile a boss that the substance of his power and control was concealed beneath a wealth of detail and unnecessary forms. In response to public condemnation or demand he could easily change a few of the outer frills without ever disturbing the central core of his control, a control so perfect and universally accepted that it did not change essentially at his death.

*Part Five*

THE NATION'S BOSS

In 1904 Matthew Stanley Quay died and Penrose was left, the imperious, unmatched, and unquestioned master of Pennsylvania politics. Very soon his mastery included the nation. Penrose, during one of the most turbulent periods of Pennsylvania's always turbulent politics, had many times been of inestimable assistance to Quay in his elections. These two men had helped each other much. Now that the master was gone there was no doubt in the minds of a single Republican politician anywhere in the country as to his successor. Penrose made perhaps the longest speech of his career in his eulogy of Quay, the occasion being the Memorial Service held in the Senate, February 18, 1905. It is much too long to quote in its entirety but a few extracts are worthy of inclusion.

"Mr. President, in addressing you today I bear my last tribute to the memory of one with whom I had held associations of peculiar intimacy, social, political, and official, for a period of about twenty years. Tested in many severe political contests, our relations were seldom marred by any disagreement, and never encountered an occasion to disturb our mutual confidence and regard.

"His character was complex, and his abilities so extraordinary as to be many times misunderstood. . . . No man in the history of American politics was so much the subject of unbridled, malevolent, partisan, and ignorant abuse and misrepresentation. Proper criticism of public men is to be invited and encouraged and not decried, but in his case criticism overshot the mark. Unjust and baseless calumny and detraction only excited the generous indignation of his friends and strengthened the adherence and determination of his party followers; while the public mind, made callous by indiscriminate abuse, gave deaf ear even when appeals were made in matters often of legitimate discussion and criticism. . . .

"In perhaps the darkest hour of his long and often stormy political career, by a courageous and aggressive movement, he struck the center of the opposition forces, and was elected Treasurer of the State. . . ."

These were years of slow but determined change, changes of tremendous political import. The Old Guard of the previous decade were slipping quietly out of the picture. In the year of Quay's death two other strong pillars of the Senate, Hanna and Hoar, died, and within five or six years thereafter such leaders as Platt, Aldrich, Allison, Foraker, Spooner, and a number of less important members disappeared from the scene. These were the same men of whom Henry Needham wrote in 1906. "The remarkable growth," he said, "of the big corporation in America has taken place in the last quarter-century. They were called into power by these men, or else have been continued in power, by the exigencies of business.

"The trail of direct purchase of seats runs into the Senate; there are senators who have been convicted in the courts of selling their political influence; there is not a great interest that has not its Senators, and so frank have these relations become that the public business has been transacted in the light of this knowledge. Debating has become a farce.

"If one lives a little while in the political atmosphere of Washington, he hears only of 'business' in connection with the Senate—political or financial business. The advent of Senators Aldrich, Hale, Frye, Spooner, Gallinger, Penrose, Platt, Elkins, Foraker, Depew, and Kean—representatives of corporate business, everyone—has produced in Washington as commercial an atmosphere, in its way, as the atmosphere of Wall Street itself."

When Roosevelt came into the Presidency Platt's hold on New York became less secure. Aldrich's power had already begun to wane, but that of Penrose had begun a steady ascent. Fortunately for the former, he had taken Penrose under his wing as soon as that young man entered the Senate, and apprenticed him to the powerful Committee on Finance, of which later he became Chairman, and also later he was given the Chairmanship of the Committee on Post Offices and Post Roads. Now Penrose could take up the reins as they were gradually relaxed by the once powerful Aldrich.

At about this same time the slow deep-moving undercurrent of unrest and bewilderment of large masses of the people was coming to the surface again, this time in different form. As the more conservative members of Congress left the scene that type of independent and progressive legislator which refused to stay hitched to the machine band-wagon, began to appear in numbers. Beveridge in 1899, defied the Indiana bosses and was elected to the Senate. So did McCumber in North Dakota, and in the next few years came LaFollette, Borah, Walsh, Norris, Capper, and an ever-increasing list of those who refused to be bound by the strict rules and practices of party.

In the realm of business significant changes were taking place which paralleled the changes in politics. In 1899 the Standard Oil Company replaced the less wieldy Trust. In the same year a dozen other large corporations were formed, chief among them were the Smelters' Trust and the Copper Trust. In 1900 the National Sugar Refining Company was capitalized at upwards of a billion dollars. In March the following year J. P. Morgan announced that the United States Steel Corporation had been capitalized at $1,100,000,000. The billion dollar corporation had come. Six months later, September 14, 1901, Theodore Roosevelt succeeded to the Presidency. The trusts had come; so had the trust-buster. His Attorney-General was the honest and high-minded Philander C. Knox of Pennsylvania. Knox at once began legal proceedings against the trusts and by 1904 he had bagged twenty-five of those lawless monsters with federal injunctions.

Roosevelt had led the pace earlier for the progressives by defying the bosses of his party in New York. Tom Platt was never able to make Roosevelt toe the mark and Penrose had lent heroic aid in the Vice-Presidential nomination matter by helping to transfer the young "jumping Jack" from Albany to Washington. Now it was Penrose who a second time could do a good turn for the same crowd—in exchange for a little assistance.

When Quay died, the Republican Organization in Pennsylvania, was in debt to the extent of some half-million dollars. Quay's name was on the notes, as were some others, among them Penrose's major political puppet in the State, the redoubtable Izzy Durham. The holders of the notes were getting a little impatient and threats of court action were heard.

Penrose's name was not on the notes but he undertook to lift the debt. It would be rather uncomfortable to be thrown into the turmoil of political bickering which a legal battle would precipitate! Furthermore, it would be inconvenient to try to force the Republicans of Pennsylvania to pay the debts of their own party. Of course there was perhaps sufficient Quay property round about to have satisfied a court order, but that would never do! Why not let those who were profiting most under the protection of the great Republican party pay the bill? Individuals had been known to pay $500,000 and more for a seat in the Senate, but at that it was seldom his own money he spent; he spent only contributions. Well, the same source of "contributions" could be tapped again! So Penrose went to New York to sell a Pennsylvania senatorship.

The exact sources consulted are not known, but rumor has it that boss Tom Platt of New York, and Senator Aldrich, father-in-law of John D. Rockefeller, Jr., helped to find the source. In fact there were quite a number of sources at the time that were willing to pay liberally to be rid of such an efficient and pestiferous Attorney-General as Philander Knox. He had already secured too many indictments. It would be worth much more than a half-million dollars to have such an energetic Attorney-General transferred to a less strategic position, some place where he would be comparatively harmless—the United States Senate, for example—and he was. Penrose came back to Pennsylvania and gave word to the boys in Harrisburg that Mr. Philander Chase Knox must be the next Senator from Pennsylvania and for them to vote accordingly. Of course Mr. Knox never knew that any such trade was made, for it is quite certain that he would not have been a party to any sort of trade that might give room for a breath of suspicion. At any rate, those troublesome notes, amounting to a good sized fortune, had been put to rest, a too meddlesome Attorney-General had been removed from the Cabinet, Penrose was happy, and Pennsylvania had a new Senator. All of which turned out just as it should in a well regulated system of bossed politics. Early in the following January, Knox, Penrose, and Izzy Durham spent a few days in Harrisburg till that obedient Legislature formally elected Mr. Knox for a full six-year term as Penrose's partner in the Senate. . . .

But Knox was not particularly happy nor brilliantly successful as Senator, so when Mr. Taft was elected President to succeed Roosevelt and took Knox back into the Cabinet as Secretary of State, he was very likely better pleased. He was not quite the same pattern as Penrose and was never a very great asset to the Pennsylvania machine, except in so far as his prestige and admitted ability helped to silence the criticism of the Penrose methods. Therefore the latter was visibly pleased when Knox again was pulled into the Cabinet as Secretary of State. In fact he was so well pleased that when, in 1910, sentiment in Pennsylvania began to gather headway to run Mr. Knox for Governor, the mighty boss, Penrose, became alarmed. Naturally he couldn't have an independent like Knox for Governor. Penrose had a long talk with Taft, who in turn had a heart to heart talk with Knox, who in turn remained out of Pennsylvania politics and in the Taft Cabinet. Again Penrose was happy.

When Quay went to Washington in 1889 he left the Pennsylvania politics largely in the hands of Boies Penrose, not as a lackey to carry out orders, but as a partner; when Penrose went to Washington he left the political scrub work in the hands of the unimaginative Israel Durham, not as a partner, but as a dependable lackey always ready and willing to carry out orders. Upon the death of Quay, and even several months before, the reins of both state and national politics slipped into the hands of the capable Penrose. He, too, was always in need of help from his clients and it was always forthcoming. Never was a feudal lord served more graciously and with greater flourish than was Penrose served by the estimable Mr. Durham, who asked nothing greater in honor than to bask in the reflected glory of the Great One. Mr. Durham was promoted from a Philadelphia ward heeler to assistant in the State and confidant of the Big Boss himself. One of his important duties was to iron out election fraud cases. It is more proper to say that his duty was to blot them out.

One such duty arose out of the election of 1899. That election was not essentially different from a multitude of other elections held in Philadelphia except for the fact that some of the important cheaters were arrested. Perhaps it was unfortunate for the Organization that a very important lieutenant, Samuel Salter, was caught directly involved in the frauds. On November 7, immediately following the election, Salter and five others were arrested and accused of stealing votes, and sundry sins. Later all were released on heavy bail. While the supporters of good clean government were congratulating themselves on at last being able to bring the election crookedness out into the open, Salter and all the other accused ballot thieves fled to foreign countries until the political barometer steadied itself. Their bail was forfeited. That, however, as it proved, was only an empty gesture, for after four years practically none of the money had ever found its way to court. During the more than four years' "leave" that these alleged crooks spent in foreign lands the Organization had to care for them, between $30,000 and $50,000 being spent for that commendable purpose.

Finally the Organization, after four and one-half years, prepared the way for the return and "vindication" of these men. First, friendly officials had to be elected to fill strategic places before a trial could be risked. Then, "just in case," they had to have the Pardon and Parole Board well padded with Organization friends. However, there must be no false step. Vindication of these accused men meant vindication for the Organization.

To get a friendly jury they had to have control of the Sheriff's office. That accomplished, they brought the accused gentlemen to trial.

The Philadelphia Public Ledger of December 4, 1904, gives an interesting story of the episode.

"Having secured a jury panel that was in every way satisfactory," said the paper, "the Organization notified Salter and the others to prepare to come into court for their vindication. Durham, according to report, then called upon District Attorney Weaver, and is alleged to have said:

"We are going to bring Salter and the other fellows back and I want them tried before Judge Davis, and during the May term, without fail."

"Why, I cannot prepare to try such an important case as theirs in so short a time."

"You must!"

"Why?"

"You do not need to know why, but it must be done."

"I can't, Iz."

"You must."

"This is awful!"

"Don't preach! You have nothing to do with this but try the case. You can make all the fight you want. You can say what you please and do what you like, but *you must not exhaust the jury panel by challenges under any circumstances* (italics mine). This is the first thing I have asked of you and it will be the last while you are District Attorney, but this one thing must be done."

"The people won't stand for it."

"You come into court and fight like hell. That will let you out. Will you do this for the Organization and for me?"

"I will do it for you, Iz, but it is certainly awful."

The trial was held in the May term of court according to schedule and all the accused were acquitted according to schedule despite large quantities of indisputable proof to the contrary. But when one considers that on the jury which "weighed" the evidence, one juror was recognized as an escaped convict from New York, and two others had prison records in Pennsylvania, one is not surprised at the verdict.

Penrose was seldom free from petty annoyance of this kind which meddlesome reformers and uplifters were always forcing to the front.

"They might as well save their energy," he told a reporter. "If people want to steal ballots or stuff boxes, that is their business and they'll find a way to do it."

He was quite correct in saying that ballots would continue to be stolen and all sorts of election frauds be perpetrated, for no one was in a better position to know the methods by which such things came about. He also knew the methods by which such thievery was protected and the thieves made immune. For example, a few months after Salter was acquitted another election was held, the city election of January 20, 1905, when incidents similar to the Salter case were recorded.

About half an hour after the polls closed and various watchers were standing over the counting to see that no mischief was done, Peter Brennan, one of the Independent leaders, was standing at the polling place and merely watching, when more than a dozen patrolmen rushed up to the scene. Eight of the men were in uniform and six of them were ordinary plain clothes men; all of them of the regular force of the city and supposedly doing duty as such.

Suddenly and without reason one of the policemen struck Brennan on the side of his head with a blackjack and knocked him unconscious. As he fell over another policeman struck him in the face to make sure that he was really and truly unconscious. Then two other policemen collared the unhappy man and dragged him to the patrol box and called the wagon. He was taken to the police station where he was booked for disorderly conduct. After a short time in a cell he was revived and released by Magistrate Ackerman for a hearing the next morning, at which time Magistrate Pullinger discharged him. By that time the ballots had all been counted, some of them twice.

There were some important arrests in the 13th ward, Sheriff James L. Miles' bailiwick, the "friendly" sheriff who had helped so valiantly to secure Salter's vindication. Four Organization workers were arrested and charged with having stuffed the ballot box, before 7 A. M., so full that when the first man arrived to vote he had to pound the ballot in with his fist, and even then it stuck out like a book mark.

Naturally Penrose was not directly connected with any such inconsequential matters as election frauds, but he was the generalissimo who directed subordinates. Nevertheless he became the target for his political enemies and all the reform elements in the State to shoot at. They knew in their own minds that he was bound up in some way with all these frauds, but to catch him was the problem. When, the next year, scandals broke with such fury over the entire Republican Organization of the State over the construction and furnishing of the State Capitol, the enemies of Penrose at last smirked in glee that they had him cornered and surely would involve him in the mess. They should have known better than to expect anything of the kind, for he was far too shrewd to allow himself to be caught in a corner.

On February 2, 1897, when the streets, houses, and fire plugs were embedded in heavy ice and snow in the coldest weather of the year, the Capitol was suddenly discovered to be on fire and it burned so quickly that the firemen had no chance to save it. It was impossible, in the bitter cold and ice, to get their hose stretched along several blocks and save the building. The Legislature was in session and they had to flee in the midst of a lot of unfinished business, leaving most of the

precious State records behind to be consumed by the flames.
Some persons then were so ungenerous as to hint suspiciously
at a mysterious fire as the best way to get rid of certain records.
At any rate, with commendable swiftness, the legislators voted
an initial fund of a half-million dollars to build the first wing
of the new Capitol. A year or two later more money was voted,
but the total amount was not to exceed four millions of dollars. But that didn't include the furnishings—merely paid for
the shell. By the time the great pile was furnished nearly nine
millions more had been added to the bill, and Pennsylvania
suddenly became dizzy. The parquetry floor for one room,
for example, as it was revealed in the investigations which
followed, could have been laid for $1800. It had cost the State
$90,000 a room—and there were four hundred and seventy-
five rooms. Chandeliers that could have been purchased for
$150 each were purchased by weight instead of the piece. All
the hollow places were filled with lead before being weighed,
and the public paid $2500 each for their chandeliers. Rugs at
$800 each wore through within a few weeks. Spittoons worth
not more than $5.00 apiece had cost the State ninety. Nothing
was overlooked. Altogether the huge building and furnishings
cost the State some thirteen millions of dollars, which was at
least eight millions too much. This was a scandal worth any
man's consideration, and all Pennsylvania considered it from
many angles.

For one thing, convictions were going to reach out and up
till all the bigwigs were brought low, but nothing of the kind
happened. Not a single important politician went to jail. The
men higher up were too smart for mere investigators and had
so worded the contracts in the first place, then manipulated
the meaning so as to eliminate anything to investigate. Only a
few innocent persons were caught, but they didn't matter.

No worse for them to go to jail than for a few bank cashiers in past years to commit suicide—all for the good of the Organization.

It was during this investigation that Penrose added to his assertions made on several occasions that he had never made any money out of politics. He was always very scornful of Quay and his sort for profiting by the petty graft in contracts and the like. Franchises, contracts, gambling with State funds, small bribes, and things of that kind, furnished the source of Quay's wealth. But why risk going to the penitentiary by picking up little amounts by graft when the real money was to be had by working for those who controlled mines and steel mills and railroads. They paid handsomely for a law passed or defeated now and then. Of course all the little fellows who got their hands into the eight-million dollar graft bag couldn't work for the big capitalists; they worked with and for the Organization, and that meant for Penrose. The fifty thousand, more or less, who lived by petty politics in Pennsylvania, had to pick up the small change where they could find it. That was the reason they were little, Penrose thought, and for that very reason he scorned them. He had a lot of contempt for small people—but he used them to make himself big. That's what they lived for—to be of use to him!

Not only were changes altering the nature of public affairs, but changes were taking place in and about Boies Penrose. Not great changes, for he was one who early ceased growing, and he never changed his method of thinking and acting, but certain slow changes which assure one that there is movement. He was now, in his late forties, accepted as the boss of the National Republican party. He enlarged his staff of assistants, which included, among other functionaries, an expert in history and politics to keep him posted in that field, another to assist visitors who came from Pennsylvania to see Penrose and Washington, and to escort them to places of interest over the city, another to collect clippings about activities that pertained to business. He employed a large variety of secretaries, messengers, go-betweens, fixers, spies, and trusties, responsible to him peronally. He accepted the duties and responsibilities of his position as a matter of course and began to conduct himself in a manner that would solidify himself with his party. He knew that politics was not a game to be played by idealists nor in the seclusion of a philosopher's retreat. He was forced always into the midst of the political whirlwind. He had no time for speculation—except in the field of human relations. In the political game every man was a pawn. He had no love for stocks or bonds unless they could readily be converted into cash of the realm. Being a political manipulator and nothing but that all his life he lived in an atmosphere of suspicion, chicanery, and double-dealing. He mistrusted everybody's motives and misinterpreted their actions. If a lady smiled at him he was sure she had designs on him of some sort—to entangle him in marriage or snare some of his wealth. To get married was to confess the weakness of having to depend on others.

Given that mental pattern it is easy to understand why he had only contempt for reformers. Having no ideals himself and believing that ideals in another were only a device handy in taking advantage of others, he held all idealists in contempt. He was utterly incapable of believing that anyone could be altruistic. He couldn't comprehend it. Politics has ever churned about in a concoction of expediency, graft, deceit, profit, and authority, and nothing better could come out of the mixture. Therefore his complete and abysmal disdain for a person like Woodrow Wilson and his "New Freedom," or for Theodore Roosevelt and his "Square Deal."

The marks of youth were now disappearing from his once

handsome person and middle age was settling into heavy folds of flesh around his enormous neck and jowls. His hands grew pudgy. His cheeks began to push out and absorb the space around his eyes and nose, and his mouth began to droop a little more definitely at the corners. His weight was considerably in excess of three hundred pound. His chair in the Senate, being of standard size, was too small to accommodate him, so he had a large divan brought in and placed at the rear of the room on the Republican side of the Senate. There he was accustomed to sit and listen in bored patience while the business of the nation was being transacted. With his great legs sprawled apart, his huge paunch resting on the upper parts of his fleshy thighs, massive shoulders pushing upward till his neck all but disappeared, rolls of fat overflowing his collar, large head resting motionless on his shoulders like a cork in a jug, beady eyes in a far-away gaze, he listened apathetically to all who had something to tell him or some favor to ask.

His huge body was matched only by his great sloth. But if one looking on doubted that there was enough energy to propel his enormous bulk, that one was sure to be disillusioned. His energy was extraordinary and the manner of its use was not only extraordinary but pathetic. With the giant intellect which he possessed, coupled with a seeming inexhaustible supply of energy, he was content to loll motionless mentally and physically till the hidden springs of power bubbled over and pushed him into action again. And that action, once he got under way, was appalling. He might have gone far had he disciplined his faculties and directed all that potential power into constructive channels, but discipline required effort, and that was something he refused to countenance. He chose to follow his appetites and let them absorb what they would.

His appetite and capacity for food and drink were almost beyond comprehension, and both grew with his age and bulk.

One who knew him well tells of the Penrose habit and prowess: "It was nothing for Penrose and Samuel P. Rotan, the late District Attorney of Philadelphia, to dispose of a whole stuffed turkey at lunch. At the Shelburne Hotel in Atlantic City there is a waiter who still tells in an awed voice of Penrose sitting down alone to a dinner of a dozen raw oysters, chicken gumbo, a terrapin stew, two canvas back ducks, mashed potatoes, lima beans, macaroni, asparagus, cole slaw and stewed corn, one hot mince pie, and a quart of coffee. All of which he stowed away while he drank a bottle of sauterne, a quart of champagne, and several cognacs. One reasonably suspects exaggeration, but waiters with similar stories are to be heard in Washington, Philadelphia, and New York.

Even better is the story of a captain of waiters in Baltimore who remembers the evening when Penrose listened to two politicians talk steadily for two hours, while he, unaided, ate a dinner which cost eighteen dollars and some cents, not including wines, the piece de resistance of which was a seven pound beef steak, an inch and a half thick, and so rare that it was hardly warm. Penrose uttered not a word during the dinner, applying himself to the food. His two companions had had their dinners and did all the talking.

His table manners, too, were distinctive. Here we have the testimony of the Honorable J. Washington Logue, Congressman from Pennsylvania. At dinner with Mr. Logue one evening Senator Penrose drank nine cocktails and five highballs and then called for food. The meal covered a wide range of foodstuffs, the feature of which was a huge chafing dish of reed birds—twenty-six birds by actual count. Spurning the plate that the waiter offered him, Penrose pulled the chafing dish to him and planting his elbows firmly on the table proceeded to consume the twenty-six. Working with both hands, left, right, left, right—and seizing them by the legs, he devoured the creatures without a pause except occasionally to shoot three fingers of bourbon. The last bird gone, he called for a large spoon with which he ate the thick bed of wild rice on which they rested. Then drinking a bowl of gravy, and doubtless feeling better, the Senator turned to other dishes."

He could consume enough strong liquor at one sitting to make half a dozen men limp for hours but he would be only mildly refreshed. He had a taste for fine liquors or cheap gin and enjoyed both equally well, depending on the occasion and the mood. And he was equally at home in the choicest bar or in the most disreputable "joint" white or black. Thus he burned up the surplus energy which always was goading him to action, and incidentally destroyed the source as well.

He was a man of wide contrasts. Besides his fondness for books and his deep love of nature, he had a nose for old manuscripts, especially those associated with the sea and pirates and explorers and privateers. He uncovered many such manuscripts, some of which he had published privately to distribute among his friends and for his own library. He usually had 150 copies made of each title.

"The Barbary Voyage of Sir George Carteret, 1638," intrigued him mightily and he had the William E. Fell Company print and bind a few copies.

"The Travels of Robert Coverte," and "A Link with Magellan, Being a Chart of the East Indies," were others he liked— all about real he-men of the sea. He much preferred to spend his time and money this way than in any other form of diversion.

The muckraking fever elicited from Penrose only cynical disgust and, when the rights and welfare of the people were mentioned, a little higher tilt of the nose was the result, for he foresaw what most observers have thought, that the great "era of good" which the people were to enjoy after the revelations of rottenness and graft, "amounted to exactly one percent gain and ninety-nine percent pure hokum."

About this time, 1905, Bob La Follette entered the Senate. Railroad regulation and control for years had been his theme song. As a result of his agitation, so it appeared, many of the railroads of the country began to create a great fanfare of trumpets as they announced that they were about to discontinue the giving of free passes. Not even a politician could get a free pass any longer! Fine! The people applauded, but that didn't get at the root of the evil which La Follette was trying to reach. It didn't get at the root of anything which needed to be got at, but it helped to create favorable public sentiment which rendered less effective the agitation for more effective control. The Pennsylvania railroad announced of its own volition that, effective January 1, 1906, no more free passes would be given nor honored. Other roads followed that lead. Some of the minor politicians fumed, for whoever heard of a real politician paying to ride on a train or a street car?

The "free pass" racket had grown to be a serious evil, as the testimony of Governor Hanley of Indiana at the time indicates. According to him the Auditor of the State of Indiana, prior to the assembling of the Legislature each time, wrote to the railways of the State requesting them to forward to him direct all passes intended to be given at that session. The reason he gave was that he had some personal interest in certain measures before the Legislature and that he would take care of the interests of the railways and his own as well with one pass instead of two. "For three weeks prior to the opening of the Legislature," the Governor said, "the office of the Auditor of the State was made a broker's office for the distribution of passes to such members of the General Assembly as would receive them."

This led one of the journals of the time to remark: "Here we have an impressive illustration of how railroads bribe the people's representatives to betray their constituents by the gift of passes. Whenever corruption crops up in government, be it in the municipality, the state, or the nation, we almost invariably find, if we look far enough, the public service companies as prime factors in the debauching of public servants."

Of course there was a flurry among certain types of politicians about what the railroads were doing to them. For years one of the most certain forms of graft to click noiselessly was that of demanding and receiving passes from the railways in return for proper attention to the railway's interests in the City Council, the Legislature, or Congress. So, they (the politicians) would show them (the Railroads) just where to get off! Local and state bosses heard the bad news from subordinates. They in turn went to Penrose. That august personage feigned hurt surprise, sniffed a great gesture, and growled.

"Humph! So that's their little game, eh?" he asked. "We'll see, damn 'em. If they won't give passes we'll make 'em give twice as big contributions to the Republican Organization—from now on."

Penrose gazed sorrowfully at the departing semi-bosses. "Poor devils!" he commented, "they do the best they can with what few brains they have." What he knew and what they didn't know was that elimination of the pass evil was more or less engineered by himself and a few high political potentates.

The gesture on the part of the carriers was not one of sentiment; it was good business. The roads would effect a considerable money savings and get better service in the bargain. Here's how it worked out! About this time a certain Western Senator, who formerly had received the support of the railway interests of his state apparently had been neglecting the interests of his clients—had not been active enough in behalf of the roads. Therefore, they notified him that at the approaching election they would throw their support to some other hired man who would be more active in the interests of his employer. That, quite naturally, meant the defeat of the senator in question. In frantic haste he appealed to Penrose. So did the railroad people. As a result Penrose promised the interests that their senator henceforth would be a railroad senator and not an uplifter—a promise which Penrose first had to exact from the harried senator. The roads were satisfied with that bargain because they knew Penrose could be depended on to keep his word, the Western Senator returned to Washington, and everybody concerned was happy. It was much cheaper for the roads to give one large contribution a year to one central committee, or a leader like Penrose, and then hold that central power responsible for results desired, than the former practice of scattering donations all over forty-six states on the vague assumption that some good might result. In the latter case the railroads would have to keep books with and watch over thousands of individual politicians and deal with each separately. In the case of centralization they could look to one man for results.

And it made the Big Boss a lot bigger. Now he could hold tighter reins than ever on United States Senator or village mayor, from Texas to Maine. Now the aspiring candidate for office had to look for support not to an individual corporation or interest but to the central boss before money and encouragement could start flowing from National Committee to State Committee to local committee. No wonder Penrose shook his head a little pleasantly at the stupidity of the lowly politician who thought the railroads had made a terrible blunder; no wonder he scoffed at the muckrakers; no wonder he smirked in complete satisfaction at his increasing power.

"Yes, sir, Iz, reform's a great blessing!"

Anti-Trust legislation, for the most part, is another example of futility. When the Sherman Act came up for amendments to make it more effective, McClure's had this to say about the original measure and its sponsors: "Senators Sherman, Hoar, Edmunds, George, and Gray: these were the men who made the present Sherman Anti-Trust law. They were the men who made largely the financial and constitutional history of the United States for the three decades following the Civil War. They brought to the consideration of the trust problems an intimate knowledge of constitutional law, an open mind, an unbiased attitude toward property rights, and a thorough devotion to public interest. They gave long and careful attention to the question, spending two years on this bill. There was nothing hasty or ill-considered about their action. They sought to end special privilege and put all citizens on the same basis of free competition. Of all great services to the nation none probably equals in importance this bill, which may be called Magna Charta of industrial and commercial liberty."

Yet, with all that preparation by the soundest minds in the United States Senate covering a period of two years, an act was put on the statute books that brought forth the above glowing tribute, but an act which added exactly zero to the common welfare of the masses. It changed the direction of the currents on the surface, at least temporarily, but it did not disturb the deeper-moving current. The Sherman Anti-Trust Act was designed to penalize combinations in restraint of trade, but it proved almost futile in that direction. It was couched in vague language and was not enforced. During the Administration of Harrison there were three indictments under the Sherman Act; during Cleveland's second term there were two indictments; in McKinley's none; during Rooseveltian days there were twenty-five and Taft nailed down forty-five. Nevertheless, during all this time the evils arising from combinations in restraint of trade have multiplied quite regularly and unrestrained. From 1895 to 1904, 5200 independent corporate businesses were merged into 372. Seemingly, though some progress had been made to the contrary, every act passed to curb corporations only increased their power, arrogance, and wealth. The political machinery was geared to the task of making that control easy, and it has succeeded beyond all expectations by following the pattern set by corporate business which prostitutes the State by first prostituting public officials. Generally speaking there have been no corrupt politicians elected to office; they have been made corrupt, after entering office, by corrupt business men and selfish interests. Corrupt officials prostitute the functions of government to enrich the same businesses which first corrupted the officials. Let one of the most noted of the idle rich of the 1890's, Frederick Towsend, Martin, speak.

"We are not politicians or public thinkers; we are the rich; we own America; we got it, God knows how, but we intend to keep it if we can by throwing all the tremendous weight of our support, our influence, our money, our political connections, our purchased senators, our hungry congressmen, our public-speaking demogogs into the scale against any legislature, any political platform, any presidential campaign that threatens the integrity of our estate. . . . We care absolutely nothing about statehood bills, pension agitation, waterway appropriations, 'pork barrels,' states rights, or any other political question, save inasmuch as it threatens or fortifies existing conditions. Touch the question of the tariff, touch the issue of the income tax, touch the problem of railroad regulation, or touch the most vital of all business matters—the question of general federal regulation of industrial corporations—and the people amongst whom I live my life become immediately rabid partisans. . . . The class I represent care nothing for

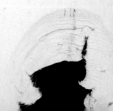

politics. In a single season a plutocratic leader hurled his influence and money into the scale to elect a Republican governor on the Pacific coast and Democratic governor on the Atlantic coast."

The same individual, speaking twenty years later, philosophized in sardonic vein about the same idea, said:

"It is always strange to me, and it has always been strange to other men who have studied those things, that a plutocracy can so long be maintained; for a plutocracy, of its very nature, is the weakest possible form of government. It lives either by fraud or force. . . . It lives in America by fraud alone; and what may we say of the people of this nation that permit it to live?"

Penrose had a way of explaining it. "The people are all right," he said, "but their tastes are simple: they dearly love hokum."

But was it hokum? Or was Penrose guilty of perpetuating the same set of fallacies which explain in part the vacuity of his public life?

The Martins may not have been interested in partisan politics but they were absorbed in the politics of acquisition and control. True, they cared not about the party label, but they were determined to insure their domination at all costs. And, as their spokesman so blandly confessed, their control has been secured and maintained by fraud alone. They found Boies Penrose an excellent clearing house for their fraudulent machinations and they bulwarked him with all their resources. He fitted well the part and brought the maximum success to it.

Penrose learned in his early Pennsylvania days that most of the people he observed, whom he called "just the average lot of folks," were only interested in what would happen to them tomorrow, that their interest extended no further than the village pump. With him all issues were local, for he knew, con-

trary to Towsend Martin's statement, that, while the rich owners of America were concerned only with the national problems of tariff, income, taxes, and federal control, the man on the street and the farm cared only for the most local of issues. That accounts for Penrose's devotion to the parochial view; he could be nearer the source of sovereignty than the statesman who forgot the musty corners and back alleys of politics. He knew that, though the country be tottering in the midst of a great crisis, more votes could be corralled in Spavin Center by talking better soy beans, an honest sheriff, and a new post office bui'ding for Spavin Center than by explaining to them a given candidate's position on imperialism or the noble aims of The Hague.

He cared nothing for what people referred to vaguely as statesmanship; he was not interested in racial problems, social issues, international questions; he was concerned solely in controlling a man's vote and controlling the actions of the recipient of that vote. His record makes rather dull reading. Scan his record for nearly twenty-five years in the Senate and one finds measured in terms of broad, national questions, the tamest sort of activity. He was a member of various Senate committees, most important of which were Coast Defense, Education and Labor, Immigration, Naval Affairs, Post-Offices and Post-roads, and Finance. He was Chairman of the last two committees. Of the bills and resolutions introduced by him we find such routine matters as bills for:

> Adams, George, for relief,
> Anderson, Peter Philip, for relief,
> Anthony, George, to pensions,
> Army nurses, to erect monument to,
> Albuquerque, N. Mex., to erect public building in,

and so on, to the end of the alphabet, sponsoring 1122 such measures in one short session of Congress, all having to do with pensions, monuments, public buildings, and the like. Nothing else.

The reader will recall one Bull Andrews, important political satellite of Boies Penrose, who went to New Mexico to fight for joint statehood for Arizona and New Mexico, so that said Andrews might have a senatorship. That explains Penrose's interest in advocating a public building in the city of Albuquerque. And that is a picture, on the public side, of Boies Penrose, concerned throughout his long public career solemnly with trivialities. His genius lay in using trivialities to accomplish big things for his party.

It was reasonable to expect at least one vote, perhaps a dozen, from every family where a pension lodged; not only a vote, but in many cases active workers for his cause. Statesmen might talk about international amity, or Chinese tug-boat scandals, or about Philippine sugar and religion, but Penrose and all the sub-leaders of the Republican party focussed attention on local problems, something the populace of that locality could understand. If one section wanted a dry river dredged, the politician, Democrat or Republican, would talk "pork" till after election day. Or, if a present incumbent of office had had marital unpleasantness, he talked sanctity of the home, motherhood—anything to draw attention away from fundamental issues. All these local issues were voted on as local issues and linked inextricably with Penrose or his star candidate for local, state, or national office. But national issues were kept in the background. Although candidates received their majorities on local issues they received their orders, once safely anchored to a payroll, from the owners of the machinery—the rich Martins, Insulls, Morgans, Ryans, Mellons, and Rockefellers— who were the only ones capable of understanding and acting on such things as tariffs, sound money, international trade, income taxes, and the like.

For more than a quarter of a century there had been under way a merciless, and sometimes, a malicious campaign, aggressive and unyielding, to create in the minds of the average laymen, a deep-seated distrust of the people. The prime movers in this campaign were those who had most to gain by successful results. They and their hired publicity agents, such as Congressman Sibley of Pennsylvania had advocated to the Standard Oil Company, spread the notion that they themselves constituted the "better element," and the "safe and sane" pillars of the Republic. The methods used in wielding their power over opinion-forming agencies, had paralyzed the great moral forces of the nation. Any person who doubted the sanctity of opinions of this "better element" were classed as the "dangerous element," and the "unruly members of society."

It became dangerous to hold dissenting opinions, even in times of peace, much less so in the shadow of war. Whatever opinion or creed the financial potentates of Wall Street wanted accepted and preached by a seeker or holder of public office, in Sacramento or Sandusky, had to be accepted. And Mr. Penrose controlled the machinery which could force the acceptance of such a creed or opinion, or retire the dissenter to private life. The individual no longer had the slightest chance in politics, and as an individual he ceased to hold office. Business set the Standard of morals and civic duty with equal impartiality. What a man might do as a business man bore little or no relation to what a man might or should do as a citizen. There were no morals in business. A man might be a robber, a pirate, or a bankrupter of small businesses, but if he "made good" and donated an art gallery to his native village he was a beneficent Christian gentleman. John D. Rockefeller was one of the most ruthless business pirates of his time, but he established some Foundations and people praised him; Andrew Carnegie sent thousands of American laborers to the bread lines in order to fill their places with more submissive and cheaper immigrant labor, thereby increasing his personal income annually to about $30,000,000, gave a few libraries, and was a patriotic American. In 1902 coal miners struck against intolerable working conditions in the Pennsylvania coal fields, wages, rat-hole houses, and starvation, and some of them were driven back to work, or to the bread lines, at the points of bayonets while the spokesman for the operators was declaring that, "the rights and interests of the laboring man will be protected and cared for, not by the labor agitators, but by the Christian men to whom God in His infinite wisdom has given the control of property interests in this country, and upon the successful management of which so much depends." The unthinking public accepted that drivel in preference to the complaints of the workers. Why? Study the methods of controlling opinion built up during the three preceding decades!

Business and politics were entirely divorced from ethical and moral standards. So was Penrose. One major difference between them was that while the former attempted occasionally to affect respectability and to repeat the pious drivel noted above, Penrose himself was beautifully free of any form of hypocrisy. He had the good grace and honesty not to form a partnership with God. Morals were all very well for persons who had time to practice them but as for him he followed his own bent regardless of standards.

His mood might dictate a ride into the country, in which case he drove in his big red automobile to the Capitol after luncheon, sent his chauffeur in for one of his friends in the Senate, told him to get into the car, drove seventy-five miles over Maryland or Virginia hills, returned to the Capitol where the Senator was dropped, and went on his way without having uttered a single word.

If one accused him of being a statesman he usually flew into a rage. He made no pretensions at statesmanship and scorned being called an expert on tariff questions or any other questions. Here was a man who never made a speech worth listening to; who, except in his early youth, seldom wrote a line about public policy; who, during his more than thirty years in public life, never sponsored a single measure of more than local interest; who denounced and fought every progressive measure in city, state, and nation; and who, from 1904 to the day of his death was more thoroughly bulwarked by financial and industrial forces than any man in public life. No man ever had greater influence in party councils of the nation than he. The nearest approach to exception to this general picture is a speech he made April 24, 1900, in the United States Senate on the "validity of the Quay appointment," and in May of the same year on "An increase in Navy Appropriations."

As for his own state, compare the long-winded, semi-barbaric, and hate-torn state conventions while Quay was in command to those same conventions run by Penrose. In 1910, the State Republican Convention met to transact the usual party business. It met, organized, was prayed for, had roll call, adopted an elaborate platform, nominated a full state ticket, and adjourned, all in one hour and ten minutes. Penrose had arranged everything in advance and his program halted at no point. Nothing more perfect and frictionless has ever been demonstrated in American politics.

His control of the State Legislature presents a similar picture. While Quay was in control there was nearly always factionalism which snarled back and forth over a thousand petty questions. Quay would threaten, plead, bribe, or bludgeon his way along somehow, but always with a tremendous lot of noise and confusion. Not so Penrose. Harrisburg ceased cringing in terror while the Legislature was in session. In fact the business of law-making went along so smoothly that few people knew what was happening. The Philadelphia Public Ledger has summed it up very nicely in giving a picture of Penrose's superb control. Nothing like it was ever seen during the Cameron or Quay dominance, nor since.

". . . Picture a pyramid. The apex is Senator Boies Penrose. His throne, inscribed with 'Divine Right of Bosses,' rests upon McNichol and Vare. Under McNichol and Vare are contractors, duel office-holders, and hand-fed leaders. These rest for their influence and immunity upon scores of lesser bosses, bosslets, boss-barnacles apportioned to the various communities of the Commonwealth. Beneath these are the wholesale and retail liquor interests, rich, astute, and unscrupulous, and levying tribute unto themselves and their disreputable dependents to fill the coffers of the dynasty above them. The next layer of the pyramid is made up of solid business men, holding their breath and shutting their nostrils, but all the while patiently bearing all, ignoring all, extenuating all, because Penrose, the reputed tariff mogul, is thought to sway the protection scepter that permits them to draw dividends and divide profits. And then under them and carrying the weight of all are the great, dear, sincere, unsophisticated but duped, God-fearing citizens who have thought so much of the raptures of the next world that they have not surmised the rottenness of this.

"For sometime Boies Penrose has ruled Pennsylvania as absolutely as the Sultan of Sulu ruled his distant domain and with about the same tender regard for the interests of his subjects. It is several generations since the people of Pennsylvania have known independence except as a Fourth of July tradition. Men who have known Harrisburg in recent decades have spoken of the members of the Legislature as pawns, which is an insult to the pawns, because a pawn can take a bishop, a knight or a castle, and can put a king in check; they have been puppets automatically obedient to the will of the Sultan of Sulu. There have been periods when the Legislature has had to mark time and the Governor look sublime in enforced idleness until McNichol could discover the will of his sovereign overlord in Washington."

Whether that type of organization and control be good or bad, depending upon the point of view, it was at least masterly. With Penrose national political control assumed that same centralized, business-like nature that his State Conventions exhibited. Business methods of centralized control were applied to politics with gratifying results—to Big Business, owners of the political machine. And this dictatorship by business grew up in a country that in theory had the widest application of the democratic principles of any nation in the world.

Being boss of the Republican Party was a man-size job. During sessions of Congress he had no time to loaf, play games, get drunk, go to the theatre, or otherwise engage in flirtations with levity; his enormous energy and keen intellect were applied without stint to the job of being boss.

He had two offices, one at his suite of rooms in the Willard hotel and the other at the Capitol office and he oscillated between them on regular schedule. The last ten years of his life he lived at the Wardhan Park hotel and he had a more elaborate office there than he had at the Willard. At both, the Senate office and the hotel office, he lived and did things on a scale in keeping with the importance of his position and one that satisfied his conception of greatness. His salary as Senator amounted to only $10,000. Allowances for secretarial help, as Chairman of Committees, and incidentals, totaled an equal amount, but that wasn't enough. Three or four clerks and secretaries were not enough for him, so when he began to expand his staff in earnest he did it on a big scale. When on one of his conference tours he found a young man who was alert and accurate about taking notes and transcribing them, he made him his private secretary. He turned over his entire senatorial salary to his secretary for full time service. Full time meant day and night. "He kept me on the job day and night," says Leighton Taylor, the secretary in question, "and because I was willing to give him all of my time is really the reason why he made me his confidant and treated me as he did. Nothing was too good for me, and I, naturally, did everything I could to facilitate his work, no matter how difficult the work or long the hours. It was common talk among his friends and mine that he treated me more like a son than an employee. I had complete charge of his affairs, and was the only one in whom he confided 100%. I lived in his house and ate at his table, had the use of his horses, cars, yachts, entree to his clubs, etc?"

Besides Taylor, he kept fifteen to twenty-five other full-time employees to buttress him with facts and service, all of which he paid out of personal funds. Approximately $100,000 a year is what it cost him to maintain his position.

His day began at 7 o'clock, before he was dressed. While dressing and having his breakfast sent up, his secretary would be putting in long distance calls, one after another, to party leaders all over the United States. The list of calls was made up the previous evening and the calling started early in order to reach the person wanted before he left his home. Eastern states were contacted first, and by 9 o'clock, Washington time, he might be talking to a very sleepy politician in California or Oregon. He had no regard whatever for the length of his conversation; no telephone operator ever dared interrupt him to tell him how long he had talked. His telephone bill frequently ran to a thousand dollars a month, seldom as low as five hundred dollars. Telegrams, too. Any length.

His breakfast period and telephoning over—he was usually

a light eater at that time of day, consuming two whole grapefruit, three slices of ham an inch thick, a pot of coffee, a quarter pound of butter, six to twelve eggs, and a half loaf of
bread—the real work of the day started. A steady stream of
congressional leaders, Pennsylvania politicians and visitors,
state and national committeemen, came to his office in his hotel
apartment. This lasted till 12 o'clock noon, except when hear-
ings were being held before the Finance Committee of the
Senate, of which he was Chairman. In this case he presided at
the hearing from 10 o'clock to 12.

Twelve noon saw him attend the sessions of the United
States Senate. He took his place at the rear of the Republican
side on his huge couch and sat there in bored silence. But not
for long. Frequently he was prodding the majority leader in
one house or the other, directing legislation into the proper
channels, or snapping into committees that were doing wrong
things or doing them not at all. He was big and lazy and
cumbersome but he turned off an amazing amount of this kind
of work. He was the generalissimo of all legislation. This occupied him daily from noon to 5 o'clock. Then, for the next
three hours he looked after his correspondence at his Capitol
office, held conferences on pending legislation, and read the
day's newspapers.

8 p. m. began his dinner hour. His lunch had been negligible.
Like breakfast, it was just a mere snack, but dinner was something to rejoice over. Two whole ducks or a five-pound steak
with a full quart of champagne or bourbon might be called the
pivot around which circulated a first class meal. He enjoyed
eating as few people did and when he sat down to a good
dinner he didn't want it interrupted by a lot of bootless conversation. It required a full hour at least of constant stoking
to fill his vast internal void which was always growing a little
larger.

About 9 o'clock his evening began and lasted till midnight. He spent this time in reading newspaper clippings, supplied by a clipping bureau, about political events, trends, personalities, and legislative matters in every section of the country. He was as well posted on the work of state legislators or city councils, from Montana to Florida, as any citizen of these faraway places. And he knew far better what their activities meant and what to do about them than did the local citizen.

He was a hungry and rapid reader, reading a whole page at a glance. His reading method amazed everyone who knew about it. He had a photographic mind and a retentive memory. He read a line at a time, with one eye-movement, reading down the page as the ordinary reader absorbs a word at a time by reading across the page. Not only did he keep his own ample library stocked with the latest books on every conceivable subject but he would send one of his hirelings to the Library of Congress with a list of from one hundred to two hundred books at a time and have them brought to his apartment. He read and smoked. Six to eight cigars every evening. His cigars were a special brand, made for the Union League Club of Philadelphia, called Scuto, and he used no other. He bought them by the dozen boxes or the crate.

Boies Penrose never enjoyed the relaxation enjoyed by others. He never attended the theatre; the seats were too small to accommodate him. Besides, he didn't want to be on "public exhibition to be stared at like an animal in the zoo." He never attended social functions, although he was showered with invitations and eagerly sought after. He played no games, indoors or otherwise, and had no love for sports and crowds.

"What a lot of fun I'd get out of sitting for hours he-hawing like a thousand other jackasses at a lot of idiots chasing each other over the lot!"

For many years horseback riding was his only form of

recreation. He was a lover of fine horses and usually kept two or three of the best to be had. Whether in Harrisburg, Philadelphia, or Washington, he took his daily ride. Usually early morning found him in Fairmount Park in Philadelphia or Rock Creek Park in Washington cantering leisurely—alone. Along about 1913 he was getting too large for comfort—either for himself or the horse—so he bought a car.

It isn't quite correct to say that he bought a car. He was perfectly helpless about making any sort of purchase; he couldn't buy himself a toothbrush. He asked a Philadelphia friend to look after the little matter of selecting a car suitable for the boss of the Republican party. The friend did. He selected the biggest touring car on the market, a Winton Six, and had it painted a screaming red. It had bright red leather upholstering, too. The car was driven to Washington by an experienced chauffeur, properly liveried, and delivered to Big Grizzly. Penrose gazed in wonder a moment at the big red machine then climbed in with a satisfied grunt.

"What's your name?" he inquired of the chauffeur.

"Walter, sir. Walter DeHaven."

"Very well, Walter, drive around town a spell and we'll give the natives a treat."

"Yes, sir! But I can't drive very far, Sir. Have to get the next train back."

"Back where?"

"Back home, Sir."

"Who said so?" growled Penrose. "You belong with the car, don't you? How much you get paid?"

Walter told him.

"Just forget it! I'll pay you twice as much. . . . Drive on, Walter!"

Walter DeHaven stayed with Penrose till he joined the war forces in 1918, then Penrose employed another Walter, Walter Mancer, who stayed at that job till the death of Penrose; it was easier to have another Walter than to learn a new name.

From that date on motoring was Penrose's only diversion.

"Every few days," says Senator Watson, "he would say to me: 'Well, Jim, let's get in my red car and go out and look at the flowers and trees.' One day I told Theodore Roosevelt about riding with Penrose and about his talking of the flowers and the birds and the trees, etc., and Teddy said that Penrose was better informed about the flora and fauna of this part of the United States than any other man in public life, and then, turning his head to one side with one of those inimitable grimaces, said: 'except me.' "

It is significant that the Republican party enjoyed its longest period of mastery during the time Penrose was welding and operating his weapons of control. During six years of Grant's incumbency the Republicans were in control of all branches of government, but in 1877 they lost the House to the Democrats, and during the next twenty years, there were only two years of undisputed control. However, with McKinley, all functions of government passed into full control of the Republicans, which mastery they maintained for thirty-six years, except for six years of Wilson.

Strangely enough Roosevelt had little or no interest in tariff issues. All during his first term in office, when nominally he was carrying out McKinley's policies, there was a good deal of agitation for tariff revision. Immediately after his election in 1904, when he ceased being a "political accident," and Congress had assembled for its short session, the clamor from minority elements increased. No man in public life was more sensitive to public sentiment than Theodore Roosevelt, so when he took notice of this clamor, it was in the form of a hint, a sort of trial balloon, that he was considering convening

Congress in extra session to revise the tariff. The Old Guard was shocked. Immediately opposition developed. Aldrich, Chairman of the Finance Committee, had already made reservations for a sojourn in Europe, but first he went to the White House. When, after a few days, Roosevelt called a few of the Staunch conservatives into conference and polled them as to the necessity of a special session their answer was what might have been expected, a unanimous and emphatic "no." There was no extra session of Congress and that ended Roosevelt's interest in the tariff issue.

At another time the President was insisting upon some trust legislation, even if he had to call an extra session of Congress to get it. The Republicans didn't like the idea of trust legislation in the first place, and they didn't want an extra session of Congress. Penrose had a conference with Senator Elkins of West Virginia, rich, conservative, and powerful, and advised him to "go see Phil Knox about it. He's got more laws now to administer than he wants. If Knox will talk to Theodore we can forget the extra session."

A few days later Elkins said to his friends: "I have just shown Attorney-General Knox enough trust legislation now on the statute books to put every concern in the country out of business. . . . I think we shall have no more insistence upon trust legislation at this session."

In one notable instance of the Republican party's crisis Penrose exhibited a very large measure of stupidity or stubbornness. Or, perhaps it was indifference. It was a crisis in the party in power precisely because the party didn't recognize any of the manifestations of a crisis. What they elected to believe was that the expressions of Roosevelt in his attempts to interpret and integrate the social trend were merely the ravings of a demagog playing to the gallery, and that the only action necessary to end the social unrest was to defeat Roosevelt and put in his stead a conservative. That course was followed with disastrous results to the party in power. And that course marked the difference between a party boss and a party leader; Penrose missed his greatest chance of being a leader.

During the first dozen years of the 20th century there was apparent to every observer a widening base of agitation which represented profound social unrest, an unrest caused by economic tendencies. Starting years before in the more remote hinterland these agitations rose into an impressive ground swell which shook the very foundations of both parties. Although the leadership of both major parties, as well as the less impressive minority groups, was confused, it became more articulate as the years advanced. Instead of allying itself with one party it cut across the boundaries of all parties and challenged the accepted dogmas in all groups. Neither of the major parties would own the agitators and radicals. It was the party's business to adhere to the traditional principles espoused only by the stalwarts in both groups, and therefore remain conservative. They resisted change and innovation, thereby encouraging insurgency.

This new social philosophy finally found its own champions, who, in every case were outside the old conservative party leadership. Woodrow Wilson, speaking for the new elements of the Democrats in 1912, was telling the people that, "The government of the United States at present is a foster child of the special interests." The progressives, in their platform of the same year, were saying: "Behind rotten laws, and preventing sound laws, stands the corrupt boss; behind the corrupt boss stands the robber interests; and commanding these powers of pillage stand bloated human greed. It is this invisible government we must destroy if we would save American institutions." Even conservative Mr. Taft, as an ex-President, said that conditions had "crystallized into a rigid control of government by great business corporations."

For reasons which were and are apparent the Old Guard, as the conservatives liked to style themselves, never took Roosevelt seriously. They didn't take this powerful social unrest seriously. During that period which produced the war with Spain, and later the muckraking fever, this same Old Guard was welding so firmly the mechanics of domination that they felt confident no storm of discontent could ever successfully challenge their supremacy. A number of the leaders of this new trend were dangerous because they had ideas that were both unorthodox and popular. Theodore Roosevelt was the first President of the United States who advocated the use of the power of government to redistribute wealth. The old line politicians of both parties pounced upon this as the rankest sort of heresy. If there had to be a contest with this type of radicalism the Old Guard felt more secure and more willing to meet it in open frontal attack than by compromising their principles. Suppose Theodore did bluster and storm—on the front pages of newspapers—about "malefactors of great wealth," that was nothing to be frightened about; he was only the President. He didn't initiate laws nor elect Congressmen to pass them. Soon the people would grow tired of Teddy and forget all about the fads and fancies of his political spasms and continue to repose their trust and confidence in that robust Republicanism or that robust Democracy that had made the nation great. The initiative and referendum, incomes taxes, popular election of Senators, inheritance taxes, and all such things, were all right to draw people's attention away from the real issues; cause them to turn their backs on the stable while the horse was being stolen by some protected scoundrel, but they should never be allowed to padlock the doors. If any subversive laws were passed by one session they could be erased at the next. If voters, perchance, were charmed away from their reservations by the braying of any "wild jackasses of the plains," they would soon tire of the strange noises and return to the corral.

"No compromising the sound principles of the old Republican party," was Penrose's dictum, and there was none.

When Roosevelt, near the end of his trust-busting and precedent-breaking days in the White House, was getting ready to hand over the reins of government to his hand-picked successor, William Howard Taft, the old conservative crowd became more and more jubilant. Soon the irritating Theodore would be out of the way and they would be relieved from so much talk about "the people" and against the trust, and business could get back to normal. Penrose remarked to a friend:

"You know, Theodore is a hell of a good sport, after all. Going off to Africa to shoot *at* lions and bears, and such things, is certainly going to give us a rest. I wouldn't be surprised if we don't all enjoy it."

Just why the conservatives were already smacking their lips in joyful anticipation of the feast not yet in sight was not apparent to all at the time. Wasn't Taft the choice of Roosevelt? And didn't everyone know that the occupant of the White House, without whose nod of approval no one in the country had a ghost of a chance, wouldn't select a successor who would fail to carry out the Roosevelt policies? What some of them didn't realize was that the genial, high-minded, honest jurist was pitifully inept at politics. Unfortunately too many people assumed that the office of President was so exalted that cheap and rancid politics would never approach its sacred chambers. But the master politicians knew all about such

things and, being an expert judge of people, they knew their
strength with Taft. They knew that their suave persuasiveness
could make the worst appear the better reason without explaining why it appeared that way. They couldn't wait for
their new chief to be installed properly before they began their
work, and it was apparent to all on March 4th. Taft's inaugural
address started the historic rift between Roosevelt and Taft
which widened with the years and made it possible for a
Democrat to occupy the White House during eight crucial
years. Roosevelt was so angered by Taft's speech that he broke
all precedent and refused to ride back to the White House
with the incoming President. It must have been something
quite out of the ordinary to cause the strenuous one to forego
the acclaim of the multitudes along historic Pennsylvania
Avenue, even if a part of that applause was for another. The
truth is that the conservative and vacillating tone of the address
disappointed and hurt Roosevelt to such an extent that he
realized much of his seven years' work would be undone within
a few months.

The Senator from steel, the Senator from tobacco, the Senator from sugar, and so on down the corporation list, were now
in the saddle and they were sure that the path ahead was cleared
of all obstructions and had no turning. The first thing they
did was to bring in a tariff measure which made the Dingley
bill of 1897 read like a free trade thesis. They tried to rush
the measure through Congress with all the blinds drawn so
that the country at large would never know what was afoot.
However, the probing of a number of mid-Western Senators
aroused such a storm of protest against the measure that the
weaker members of the Old Guard became alarmed. This bill
caused the first open break in the Republican ranks. Ten
prominent mid-Western Senators—Beveridge, Burkett, Bris-
tow, Crawford, Clapp, Cummins, Dolliver, Brown, La Follette,

and Nelson—refused to vote with the majority for the bill, thereby reading themselves out of the party, and out of public life, so said the regulars. The country thought differently. Taft in order to justify himself before the country, protested some of the schedules, for example, the schedule on gloves. The committee on Finance, led by Aldrich, Penrose, and others, very graciously bowed to the President's wishes, lowered the tariff on gloves and raised it on a hundred other articles. Whereupon the genial President claimed a great victory, proceeded to read the progressives out of the party, or tried to, and gave a rousing "victory" dinner. Heading the list of guests were Penrose, Hale, Aldrich, Lodge, Knox, Cannon—generals all in the march back to conservatism. And in token of mellow friendships and good political fellowship, some extra fine wines, whiskies, and sherry were among the drinks. In the words of a guest at the dinner, "The President's cup raneth over."

A short time after this event the President had as his distinguished guest the noted steel magnate, Henry Clay Frick, whose business had fared so handsomely in the tariff schedules. Penrose had seen to that.

"The people don't know what they want," that enormous Senator from Pennsylvania had said. "They have to be told what they want, then we have to lead them to recognize it when they get it."

That attitude was typical of the Penrose breed and school. It explains why the rumble of discontent arising from the farms pinched by the agricultural revolution beat its tomtoms in vain; why the seething unrest of industrial masses, bludgeoned into silence by the minions of law, cried out in wave after wave of despair at seeing the fruit of their honest toil extracted from them; why coal miners, sinking ever deeper into economic helplessness, joined other forces of discontent and beat in vain against the citadels of power and privilege. It helps to explain why he was always deaf to appeals for some token of social amelioration. He and his group firmly believed, or pretended to, that the masses really had no grievances and that such hubbub as was heard from time to time, was generated by professional reformers for their own benefit. Senator Conkling of New York had summed up their attitude by saying that the cussed reformers were only "man-milliners, the dilettanti and carpet knights of politics, men whose efforts have been expended in denouncing and ridiculing and accusing honest men. . . . They were wolves in sheep's clothing whose real object is office and plunder."

Although Roosevelt was given to impulsive action and snap judgment, although he was a good deal of a poser and liked nothing better than to strut in the limelight, and although he was at heart an aristocrat playing the role of champion of the plebeian and downtrodden, he gave voice and integration to the popular unrest throughout the country. He dramatized the "Square Deal." He made insurgency respectable, and gave a powerful impetus to the hopes of millions for a realization of Bryan's fervent prayer, "Let the people rule!"

The average wage earner, farmer, clerk, or professional middle-class voter had for years vaguely sensed that the road along which one sought life, liberty, and happiness became more rugged and slippery as the years advanced, and that for some unaccountable reason the people's government had given away the people's rights to travel that public highway to a few designing individuals who had erected countless numbers of toll gates. The luckless commoner had to pay a great price to pass any one of the toll gates. He was at the mercy of the gate keepers. For some reason these keepers were a cruel and stubborn lot, bereft of understanding and vision, and they seemed to take fiendish delight in baffling and defeating the aspiring traveler. The millions of travelers, having the obedience and docility born of poverty, merely trudged on in bewilderment, and times without number, not being able to pass all the gates, were forced to turn back in bitter disappointment only to realize at last that their strength was now waning and their visions lusterless and barren.

During his nearly eight years in the White House Roosevelt preached social democracy day in and day out, and lashed into a fury popular indignation against the gate keepers. All of which caused Joseph G. Cannon, Czar of the House, to exclaim in a rage to President Taft: "I'm getting damned tired of this everlasting yielding to the popular outcry against wealth." So were all the Old Guard outraged at the clamor. Penrose always made a wry face and imitated motions of vomiting every time he discussed Teddy— All because he couldn't control Roosevelt.

Probably Roosevelt's greatest contribution to the general welfare was to dramatize the concept of robust Americanism, which in different measure meant the courage to defy the gate keeper. If that average person was somewhat hazy as to the methods of procedure, at least he was made conscious of his stake in the battle.

All of this meant nothing to Penrose. Nothing at all. He had heard the mutterings of discontent ever since that day in the early eighties when he launched himself, full-blown, into the slime of ward politics and discovered for his own satisfaction that there were only two classes in America—the rulers and the ruled. Of course the ruled always had complained about everything in sight but when given a chance to rule they were not equal to the responsibilities. He chose to move among the rulers and built up his system accordingly, a system that has for years been the marvel of big and little politicians alike. Years later (June 23, 1926) the New Republic said that "the

Pennsylvania system—of Penrose, Vare, Pepper, Mellon—is being raised to the dignity of an idea."

Roosevelt was an accident which didn't happen often, and naturally no machine or method is entirely accident proof. But it shouldn't happen a second time. A politician never leads public opinion, he follows it; a statesman never follows public opinion, he anticipates it; a boss never listens to public opinion, he merely ignores it. At least that was the Penrose dictum.

It meant nothing to him that since he entered public life in the early 1880's there had been a steady march of reform, or progressive measures, placed on the statute books, including the secret ballot, direct primaries, tariff commission, commerce commission, anti-trust legislation, direct election of United States Senators (in some states), and a multitude of lesser measures designed to place the actual government nearer the people. But had they?

"The great Republican party is still in power, as you see, and the great interests that make all these luxuries for you objectors to enjoy, and pay wages to all these workers, pay wages because the Republican party is in power. Get that, will you? They support that party. Where's the crime? And we intend to keep right on in power."

So the insurgent Senators who parted with the Taft policies, the rebellious members of the House who forced Cannonism to relax its rules, the thousand and one irritants—pricks from liberal newspapers and periodicals—and defections from the ranks, meant nothing to the bosses. Aldrich was saying in the Senate: "The Republican party is a party of majorities, and the view of the majority in matters of legislation control party policies and governmental policies."

What he didn't realize, or wouldn't admit, was that the majority in Congress, or in state Legislatures, or in City Councils, seldom represented a majority of the voters; often quite the reverse. A few thousand petty bosses, acting for the few larger bosses, in possession of a few thousand ballot boxes could nearly always be depended on to express the popular "will." Therefore the popular will could be bent and adjusted to fit the needs of the hour. Why, then, all this fawning and kow-towing to noisy clamor? When the old masters of the ruling classes wanted something they usually knew precisely how to get it. At least it had always been true and they saw no reason to doubt that it would always be true to the same principle.

So, when the end of the Taft Administration drew near, and large groups in the Republican camp were disturbed by the serious defections in their ranks many of them were saying that they could never stand another four years of Taft. The more courageous of the progressives were determined to put an end, once for all, to the dominations of a few who were responsible only to themselves or to such a small fraction of the people.

"We'll see!" roared the Old Guard, and went ahead with their preparations to nominate for a second term the pliable Mr. Taft. By liberal use of federal patronage, and various other devices, used as a whip over the progressive element who were whooping it up for Roosevelt, Taft garnered enough delegates to insure his nomination. Even this would have failed had not the bosses "disqualified" some 250 odd of the Roosevelt dele-gates through denial of their credentials. Whereupon Roose-velt requested 340 or more of his delegates not to vote, and Taft was nominated by a rump convention.

Penrose was too shrewd a politician to have any illusions about Taft's chances for re-election, even if nominated: he was convinced long before the convention that a second term for Taft was out of the question. He was just as certain that Roosevelt, if regularly nominated, could not be defeated. But he was such a stickler for regularity, which could always be dominated by the bosses, that he would rather lose with a regular like Taft than to win with an irregular "jumping Jack" like Teddy who wouldn't play ball with the boys in the accepted fashion. Penrose preached to his group that "if it's a question of losing the election or losing control of the party, lose the election." He reasoned that with another four years of Roosevelt the control of the bosses might be permanently shattered, but that a Democratic regime would in four or eight years so irritate the real ruling element and make enough fumbles to return the Old Guard to power more firmly entrenched than ever. Four years more of Roosevelt and the Old Guard would all be in padded cells! So it was determined weeks ahead of time to nominate a "safe" candidate.

Several days prior to the Republican National Convention which met June 18, 1912, in Chicago, there was a meeting of a few of the leaders, who composed an unofficial Board of Strategy, the membership of which included Boies Penrose of Pennsylvania, Reed Smoot of Utah, Jim Watson of Indiana, Uncle Joe Cannon of Illinois, Speaker of the House, William Barnes and Elihu Root of New York, Murray Crane of Massachusetts, and Nicholas Murray Butler, President of Columbia University. The principal question at issue was whether to give way to Roosevelt, throw the support of the regular organization to him and insure his election, thereby saving the party, or to wreck the party by supporting Taft whom they knew could not be elected. The latter, if elected, would please the powerful interests whose representatives most of these conferees were; the former would give them four years of back talk and denunciation. Neither course was a pleasant one. Gloom, according to one of the participants, was the most prominent aspect of the conference, besides tobacco fumes. Talk was jumpy and irritable. Long periods of silence were broken occasionally by catty remarks. After some hours of bitter wrangling, Uncle Joe Cannon remarked rather curtly: "Hell! Haven't we wasted enough time? If we are going to surrender to Roosevelt why not call him in and get our orders now?"

Penrose was pacing the floor, his huge bulk more impressive than ever. He turned to the others, his eyes smoldering, and said:

"No compromise, gentlemen! The great party will stand on the principles of its founders; to compromise at this time is eternally and everlastingly wrong. The people of this country are tired of this great Republican Party. They are tired of organization in Ohio. They are tired of bossism in Indiana. They're tired of Boies Penrose. They're tired of Joe Cannon. They're tired of the whole damned lot of us. We're going to lose this election; for God's sake let's not lose control of ourselves.

"There's only one way to go and that's straight ahead. I know damned well the road we're on leads straight over a precipice, but let us drive this grand old party to the brink. Let us drive it to the very edge, let us push it over the precipice, and then go to the other side and gather up the fragments and out of them build a new Republican party with new principles to meet advanced conditions."

And with that pronouncement the fate of the party was sealed. Afterward, with the remark that he was going to let the country forget Boies Penrose for a while, he turned his attention resolutely to his own State and his beloved city, Philadelphia, where he could find the best drinks and his favorite places of amusements and recreation.

*Part Six*

TWILIGHT ZONE

PENROSE notoriously was a hard loser, but it was not as a defeated politician that he returned to Philadelphia. His domination of that city was being threatened by the Vares. The state was none too secure, either, but he knew that if he put in a reasonable amount of hard work the opposition had no chance whatsoever in city or state. And when aroused the amount of "work" he could turn off was prodigious.

In the quiet of his Spruce Street home, with no one to dispute his supremacy except his ancient housekeeper, he had leisure to reflect on his status and the influence that one Boies Penrose might have exerted on National affairs had it not been for one Theodore Roosevelt. The Democrats, amidst the time-worn policies and the dusty bric-a-brac of the former Republican regime, were acting as the proverbial bull in a china shop; they were scattering precedents and policies and such things about the premises with abandon. They were rearranging all the furniture, and there was no telling what things would be like before they finished.

But every time he thought of the Democrats Penrose heaved a big sigh of regret—disgust. They would be in power four years! Possibly eight! By that time Penrose would be near sixty years old. Perhaps too old and fat to be of much use. Well, let's see, now! Sixty was not so old! A lot could be done after that to make life miserable for his opponents—and there would be a mighty lot to be done! By that time the country would be good and sick of "schoolmarm" Wilson and his fool theories, the big interests would be lean and hungry, and the Old Guard would be welcomed back with open arms. The prodigal son would be feasted and, though perhaps not repentant, he would give more decent heed to parental wishes—for a while.

Probably no man despised the Democrats quite so systematically and ineffectively as did Penrose. He hated the austere Wilson and his high idealism and seldom spoke of him without a sneer. He took little or no official notice of the large program of progressive measures being enacted by the Democrats. He turned his ample back on the whole procedure, except to criticise, and he was such an implacable foe of the opposition party that his criticisms often degenerated into the cheapest sort of fault finding.

He probably didn't realize it but he had reached the peak of his power and was descending on the other side. But it was not all loss. He had more time now to indulge his appetite and really give more attention to his favorite amusements. What was the need to scurry around and hold wordy conferences about the defeated party so early in the game? The Democrats were in power, weren't they? Let them do all the conferring and worrying, and let them worry the country, too! Postmortems over lost games never did anything but raise hell! Four years from now would be plenty of time to do all sorts of committee work, and things like that. In the meantime Penrose would relax and drink and eat—and grow more pudgy. And sulk! That's mostly what it amounted to. Perhaps his health was a wee bit off, too. His outraged stomach rebelled, at fifty, and occasionally refused to hold such quantities of liquor. It soured! So did his temperament. His malignant throat trouble was becoming more irritating each day and the bullfrog rumble he gave forth in trying to clear obstructions became more and more unpleasant.

He regularly made the rounds of his favorite hotels, and after the 1912 defeat, increased the frequency of his visits. He liked to go where well-trained waiters who knew how to serve a first class meal recognized him and treated him with the deference due one of his importance. They were happy when he entered the dining room, for his orders as well as his tips were liberal. His hotel in New York was the Waldorf-Astoria; in Atlantic City it was the Shelburne; in Pittsburg, the William Penn. In Philadelphia he stayed at his old home, 1331 Spruce street, and though it was kept continually manned by a full corps of servants, he seldom took his meals there. He ate at the Union League Club—the waiters there were more cheerful and liberal.

One measure, however, not initiated by the Democrats but became a law in the early months of their regime, helped Penrose more than he was willing to admit, and perhaps more than he realized. That was election of senators by popular vote. His opponents had frequently said that if he had to submit his case to the people he would be retired overwhelmingly at the first election. So, when in 1914 Penrose had to stump the State in his own behalf, the nation was more than usually interested in the outcome.

He approached that campaign in fear and trembling, for his opponents might be right about his being retired at the hands of the electorate. It had been twenty-five years since he had really mixed face to face with the electorate. A lot of changes had taken place since he was master in person at Harrisburg. For once he faced a situation which he felt was much beyond his depth. In fact he had fully made up his mind not to run for re-election and confided as much to some of his friends. He was becoming reconciled to thinking of Boies Penrose in terms of a private citizen. Before he could announce his withdrawal from the race, however, Joseph R. Grundy, President of the Pennsylvania Manufacturers' Association and high priest of the high tariff shoguns, went into action to keep Penrose in the race. Grundy told Penrose that the interests of

the State demanded his continuance in the Senate and that
they were lined up solidly for him. Penrose feared the verdict
of the popular vote and held back, but the eloquence of the
corporations, speaking through the Manufacturers' Association, overcame that fear, and Penrose entered the race.

He also feared the Vares in Philadelphia, but when the interests spoke even they could be reasonable. A very nice bit of
smart politics featured the race. The Vares promised to support Penrose in turn for the right to name the candidate for
Governor. Their candidate was Grover M. Brumbaugh, well-
known educator of the city and state. Penrose had learned
to hate the honest school teacher while he was the efficient
Superintendent of City Schools of Philadelphia because he
fought to keep the schools free from political domination.
That was enough to arouse the undying hatred of any self-
respecting politician. But now he was ready to do an about-
face and politically embrace the honest school master, for Penrose shrewdly realized that at the moment the scholar in politics
was in high favor. Woodrow Wilson was riding the crest
of popular favor. Why not capitalize on the popularity of such
a partnership, more especially since Brumbaugh had a very
strong following in the state. So, Penrose very graciously used
the upright Brumbaugh as highly attractive window dressing
for his own senatorial aspirations, swung into step with the
parade, and was re-elected to the Senate.

It was during this campaign that Penrose was forced to make
his first appeal to the people for popular support. Since he was
forced to do a little electioneering on his own account, he
certainly knew how to do it! And he would make a thorough
job of it, too!

"Well, Taylor, get your hat and jump into the car. We're
headed for the sticks."

"Pennsylvania?" asked the unprepared secretary.

"Pittsburg . . . and all the other towns that's worth a damn."

His decision and action in this matter was thoroughly Penrosian. He never gave his secretary nor his chauffeur a moment's notice about any intended trip. They had to be prepared always at a moment's notice for an unexpected trip of ten miles or a thousand; for an hour or for a month, departing any time of day or night. He had been accustomed to doing that sort of thing when he travelled on trains, so why should he change now?

So the Penrose entourage in the big red car pushed northward over the Maryland hills into Pennsylvania. It was mid-August when the first trip was made, harvest time for many crops, or past, and rural folk and small town folk had much leisure and many local fairs, carnivals, and the like. As the rolling hills and valleys in all their matured mellow foliage, meadows, and bountiful harvests greeted them, Penrose found a strange new interest in all things about him. He developed a friendly mood and had a thoroughly good time.

Gettysburg was his first stop. Not only did he have a pleasant meeting with party leaders but he found occasion to be immensely pleased otherwise. The fame of his red car had already preceded him and when he parked it in front of the hotel people stopped to gaze at it. Here was something new and interesting and attractive. When finally he emerged from the hotel the car was swallowed up in a huge admiring throng. With all the dignity of an oriental potentate Penrose pushed his way through the jam and climbed aboard. The crowd cheered. Before the end of his fall campaign his car was recognized by every urchin in the state. It could be seen a mile away. When he approached a village the youngsters would begin yelling: "Here comes Senator Penrose."

"Hiya, Senator! Fine car y' got."

"Gonna make a speech here, Senator?"

"Jeez, he's a big man!"

Penrose looked neither to the right nor the left but accepted the plaudits of his young admirers in true aristocratic style, looking straight ahead.

He confided later that when he first saw "that damned red fire wagon," he was on the point of not accepting it, for he was never given to flashy colors. But he soon realized he had an unexpected political asset of considerable value. He had many cars after that, every one an open touring car painted the same bright red. The only exception was the last car he purchased, a few months before his death. It was a black limousine.

During that first popular senatorial campaign in the autumn of 1914 he travelled more than 50,000 miles over Pennsylvania, carrying his plea for votes into the remotest byways of the state. He drove from Philadelphia to Pittsburg, over the Alleghenies and return, a distance of 610 miles, seven times in the month of October. And that was before the era of hard roads. On one trip the motor was overheated, the bearings went bad, the brakes burned out, and a short circuit caused the car to burn. They had to finish that trip by train, but immediately upon arrival at Philadelphia he purchased another car—a bright red one. In this first State-wide primary campaign he was scheduled to speak at hundreds of places and functions, among them to a monster outdoor picnic crowd near Mechanicsburg. E. J. Stackpole, a newspaper man on tour with the candidate, gives his impressions of Penrose in his new role as follows:

"It was to be a big day for the Senator. His friends were anxious that he should make a good impression on his first hunt for votes in the wide spaces and face to face with the men, women, and children of the rural districts. But they were worried without cause. Instead of any least show of embarrassment or curiosity concerning his bucolic environment, Penrose joyfully entered the large grove where thousands had assembled and soon was in the midst of such a hand-shaking bee as had never been dreamed of in his philosophy. All ages and sizes and both sexes were represented in the assembly and everywhere was an earnest desire to speak to the distinguished visitor. I never saw him happier. Without wife or child and a confirmed bachelor, he walked up and down the congested avenues shaking the hands extended to him from every direction and chatting with all, not failing to compliment the proud mothers of babies held up for his admiration. Cheers frequently greeted him as he made his way through the crowds toward the pavilion where he was to speak. His address was admirably suited to the occasion. . . . That speech stood him in good stead for years."

After his arduous but successful campaign in 1914 he felt the need of relaxations at his lodge in Florida. But the St. Lucie Club, the "Last Man's Club" organized some fifteen years previous, for political pow-wows, hunting, or carousing, was no longer of any interest to him; the Vares were charter members. And he couldn't think of them without performing another masterpiece of cursing. In the campaign just ended they had delighted themselves at his expense by winning from him the control of Philadelphia. At the time of organization of the club those estimable brothers were astride the Penrose bandwagon and worshippers at the Penrose political shrine—and incidentally learning his technic, but now—

"Damn 'em! No use trying to play ball with them any longer."

Accordingly, Boies Penrose and his three brothers, Charles, Richard, and Spencer, together with a dozen prominent Philadelphians, organized the High Point Rod and Gun Club about twenty miles from Palm Beach, Florida. This was a much more elaborate affair than the former club and it made more concessions to social amenities. It was a swanky and very exclusive outfit. Here Boies Penrose spent the remainder of his vacations.

In little more than a year after the Democrats assumed control of national affairs the Great War broke over Europe and we at once declared our neutrality. After that Penrose was not so much in the criticising mood; he was in accord with neutrality. It was a very profitable policy. His important constituents, steel for example, were piling up enormous profits. So were the great textile manufacturers. Such incidents as the Lusitania didn't cause him to move a patriotic muscle of his stolid face. Coal operators in Pennsylvania were making profits of two hundred and fifty percent in their business. Steel magnates were piling up hundreds of percent profit, so why quibble about other issues of the war?

And yet he did quibble. Two important characteristics of the man, thrown into bolder relief because of the war and its accumulated incidents, deserve a more detailed treatement here. One was his sheer honesty and freedom from anything resembling hypocrisy. He hated dissimulation and pretense and made a fine point of rebuking such unholy traits in others. Some of his closest friends and associates declare that they never heard him use the word "patriotism" except in a cynical allusion to some one, at least in no important sense, during a period when the word was being severely overworked.

An incident happened in the early stages of the War which is revealing of his sensitivity to hypocrisy. Senator La Follette bared his heart and soul in his fight against a declaration of war. Failing in that he fought bitterly against conscription. That was too much. The country demanded his political execution at once. The Senate set aside a day to expel him and to stage a Roman holiday of patriotic fervor. La Follette was almost alone in his stand. When he entered the Senate on the fateful day he was the loneliest soul in Washington. Hate-filled eyes burned into his. Weary, sick at heart, bloody but unbowed, he was a pathetic figure. When Penrose saw him he lurched to his feet, went to the side of the Wisconsin Senator, placed his arm about those heavily burdened shoulders, and walked down the Senate aisle thus. A strange hush fell over that passion-filled assembly. Penrose's act was silent notice to the patriotic world that the boss of the Republican Party would stand for no such nonsense as expulsion. La Follette was not expelled. Sentiment? Not at all! Just sheer honesty. Why not let every fellow think and act as he pleased. Speaking of patriotism, what about all those fellows in the training camps ready to go to the trenches? They were the ones who were patriotic. As for the rest of the shouters they mostly interested themselves in maintaining the security of Allied bonds. If we didn't have several billions of dollars invested in Europe to be saved from default how patriotic would some of the Senators be?

As for himself he was perfectly willing that we should fight Germany, but let's be honest about it! Nothing very patriotic in the whole mess—except in the mind of George Creel—just good business. He was opposed to all war talk till along in 1916 when it became apparent that the Allies might crumple, in which case our loans to Europe wouldn't be worth a thin dime! Then and not till then did he favor war to save our investments and profits and markets. Make the world safe for Democracy? Hell! What's democracy? Whose got it? More than that, who wants it?

Then there was the incident of the Archbold letters concerning a certificate of deposit for $25,000 sent to Penrose from the Standard Oil Company. Sure! Mr. Penrose accepted the $25,000 from the Standard Oil Company, maybe a lot more, but what of it? It was for campaign expenses. He would accept money from anybody for that purpose and in any amount, for it cost a lot of money to run a campaign. Nevertheless, those who claimed to be horribly shocked at the revelations, brought out by their publication in a widely read magazine, of correspondence proving beyond any doubt that money was being used almost openly and abundantly to influence legislation, were demanding a thorough investigation. Penrose arose to the occasion and began demanding an investigation of the campaign expenditures of the last election. "Perhaps Mr. Roosevelt—" but the demand for an investigation soon began to cool down to a mere simmer. Penrose never explained anything further about those letters, never tried to, and was not expelled—not even censured. Why pick on him when others collected and spent money for campaigns? Why not be consistent?

He kept many records of little forgotten incidents of others with which to trip them, especially when they assumed superiority in ethics or morals. He was jealously interested in the great textile industry of Pennsylvania. Frequently there was heard from some quarter stories about sweatshop conditions which were deplorable. On one occasion a certain Senator was prepared to launch an investigation into alleged textile slaves— conditions of their labor, their wages, and other unholy practices, or at least was using a threat to gain a point.

"Very well," said Mr. Penrose. "A few years ago the distinguished Senator was interested in defeating the Pure Food and Drug Act. Perhaps he would like for me to tell this body why he opposed it?—"

That was sufficient to quiet the Senator whose best constituent stood to lose a million dollars by not being allowed to sell any more tainted meats for fresh meats.